The Last Portrait: A Psalm For Monique

"Keep the Faith"

The Last Portrait: A Psalm For Monique

A Memoir by

Deborah Nelson

Copyright © 2016 Deborah Nelson
All rights reserved.

ISBN-13: 9781539636410
ISBN-10: 1539636410

Table of Contents

Acknowledgements · vii
Introduction · ix

Chapter 1	School of Hard Knocks ·	1
Chapter 2	My First Angel ·	7
Chapter 3	Life's a Mystery ·	10
Chapter 4	A New Life, A Family of My Own · · · · · · · · · · · · · ·	13
Chapter 5	We Will Love Our Children Into Excellence · · · · · · · · ·	23
Chapter 6	A New Member of the Family · · · · · · · · · · · · · · · · ·	37
Chapter 7	A Carousel of Changes ·	43
Chapter 8	Are You There? ·	55
Chapter 9	That Rogue Heart of Mine · · · · · · · · · · · · · · · · · · ·	66
Chapter 10	Nuttier Than a Fruitcake or Sweeter Than Honey · · · · · ·	80
Chapter 11	The Beginning of the End ·	89
Chapter 12	Fine As Wine ·	95
Chapter 13	A Clean-Cut Case ·	109
Chapter 14	The Rippling Effects of Street Violence · · · · · · · · · · · ·	116
Chapter 15	Change Is Not Part of My Persona · · · · · · · · · · · · · · ·	122
Chapter 16	The Scales of Justice Weigh Heavily On All · · · · · · · · ·	127
Chapter 17	A Convoluted Animal ·	132
Chapter 18	The Bottomless Pit ·	140
Chapter 19	Never Having Said Goodbye · · · · · · · · · · · · · · · · · · ·	147
Chapter 20	Special Bonds ·	157

Chapter 21	A Psalm For Monique	164
Chapter 22	Many Paths	169
Chapter 23	Moving Forward	173
Chapter 24	Final Thoughts	177
	Appendices	187
	Appendix A	189
	Appendix B	192
	Appendix C	194
	Appendix D	196
	Appendix E	198
	Appendix F	200
	Appendix G	201

*For the sake of privacy, some of the characters names have been changed.

Acknowledgements

For the loves of my life; Tamora, Anthony, Grandbabies, Family and Friends

In Memory of Monique Roxanne Nelson
January 17, 1980-December 14, 2010

A humongous thanks to my cherished family and friends who have been my backbone as we weathered this storm together. Words cannot express my heartfelt appreciation in helping to keep Monique's memory alive and embracing the life she shared with us all.

And a special thanks to Peggy Williams, the editor of this memoir. The journey was long and revealing but it provided me with a much needed pastime. Hope!

"The roots of all goodness lie in the soil of appreciation for goodness."
(Dalai Lama)

Introduction

"I am here to tell you about a vivacious, beautiful quick-witted young woman named Monique Roxanne Nelson..."

THE COURTROOM SAT HUSHED AS I read the Victim Impact Statement on behalf of my family at the sentencing of the men who murdered my precious daughter. As a mother, it was unfathomable to think that I would ever have to read such a thing. It is equally incomprehensible to think that my dear Monique is gone, that her own child is motherless, that I will never experience the joy of seeing her smile again, and that my life and the life of my family is forever changed—because of one brutal incidence of violence. But that is my reality. And it has been a nightmarish journey.

On Tuesday, December 14. 2010 I clocked out from my hospital volunteer job at 2 p.m. and rushed home to take a nap. I had promised Monique that I would baby-sit two-year-old Jayden, my grandson, that evening. As I lay on the couch cat napping, my cell phone rang.

"Mama…"

Whenever he has bad news, my son Richard takes a long series of breathy pauses before speaking. "Mama. (*pause*) Something bad has happened. (*pause*) To Monique. (*pause*). Something really, really bad…" Another long pause.

"What?" I asked. "What happened?"

That's when he stated the unimaginable. It must have been heart wrenching for him to have to tell his mother that his baby sister—her youngest child—had been caught in the crossfire between rival gangs.

Tensions had been escalating for weeks between two gangs. When members of one were spotted inside Fly Cuts & Styles, a Sacramento barbershop, members of the other swooped into the shop with their guns—a Tech-9, an AK-47, and a .38 caliber handgun—blazing.

Monique had just come out to the parking lot outside the barbershop and was buckling Jayden into his car seat. They had been at the one-hour photo shop next door having their annual Christmas portrait taken. When the gunfire broke out, she instinctively laid her body across her son.

"She was and still is deeply loved by a host of family and friends, but there was no greater love than the love she had for her rambunctious two-year-old son, Jayden."

It wasn't long after the smoke cleared and the culprits had run from the scene of the crime that police officers and first responders arrived. Trying to protect as much evidence as possible, they placed yellow crime scene tape all around and triangular markers next to bullet casings. A weapon was discovered that had been discarded on the ground. Investigators quickly rounded up potential witnesses who could help the authorities gain a better understanding of what had transpired.

Looking for additional witnesses, one investigating officer noticed the back passenger door of a Chevy Tahoe opened and a young woman leaning into. He called out to her repeatedly, to no avail. He later reported that an eerie feeling overtook him as he slowly approached the back door of the SUV. He could see that something was terribly wrong. The young woman had blood dripping from her mouth and nose and he realized that the rage of violence in the parking lot had claimed another victim—my daughter, Monique.

"... Monique worked diligently to provide for her child, made plans for their future and built a value system of family traditions that have been handed down from one generation to the next."

The Last Portrait: A Psalm For Monique

The police officer was shocked to see a two-year-old toddler in the car—under her body, still strapped into his car seat. My grandson was crying softly but was physically unharmed. His mother's body had protected him from a certain death. The officer slowly lifted Monique's lifeless body and laid her on the pavement next to her car. Firefighters rushed to her aide, but their efforts to revive her were fruitless.

Street violence has reached epidemic proportions in this nation. There is no geographical, racial, gender-oriented, age, social economic or religious group that is immune from this clear and present danger. According to the website www.bradycampaign.org, approximately 300 children and adults are victims of gun violence daily in the United States, and more than eighty-five children and adults die each day from gunshot wounds. But no one expects it to happen to their family. I never, in my worst nightmares, imagined it could happen to my child and my grandchild.

A Black Hole is a region of space and time where gravity is so strong that nothing can ever escape from it, not a ray of light, not a particle of hope. When my daughter was murdered, I entered a Black Hole. I lost my joy. I lost my bearings in life. I lost all of my spiritual and religious connections. And I nearly lost my family because of my inability to move forward.

This is the story of my descent into the Black Hole of grief due to gun violence and of my fight to escape being lost forever. I write it so that others can know there is hope. So that others can know there is a way out of the blackness that is grief, even though grief—like the Black Hole—will never stop tugging at the heart.

And I write it for Monique. For her spirit. Her laughter. Her joy. Her legacy. She died fighting to keep her baby boy alive. I write this to keep her alive.

CHAPTER 1

School of Hard Knocks

MY FIRST ENCOUNTER WITH INNER city youth similar to the ones who murdered my daughter occurred on the north side of Milwaukee, Wisconsin in the early 1960's. I was eleven years old. My mother had just left my father, and she and I had relocated from the small rural community of Davenport, Iowa where we'd lived a very traditional life.

Davenport had been a nice place to grow up in the 50's. Religion, high moral standards, and not "sparing the rod" were the rules from house to house. We were a so-called middle-class Black family living in a town of predominantly German heritage. Although my parents argued a lot, they provided my two sisters, Ellouise and Beatrice, my half-brother, Wendell, and me with a wonderful childhood full of food, laughter, and music. Education was the key. My father, Harold Lenzie Toney, was a Baptist minister, and my mother, Beatrice Hamer Toney, was a music teacher. Mother had a pure contralto voice, the genes of which she passed on to me, and ultimately on to my daughter Monique.

The Black community in Davenport was small, but we united with other Black communities in the Quad cities. In many Black homes there were three pictures on the wall: President John F. Kennedy, Martin Luther King, and a Black Jesus. A progressive city, there were many Black entrepreneurs in Davenport, and we had three Black radio stations. Although my family had money and standing, we were always reminded of our color. I was usually the only Black child in a classroom. I can remember having to fight at school for my sister Ellouise, who inherited my father's darker complexion. Beatrice and

I were lighter skinned so we received better treatment. That used to anger me to the hilt.

In the 1960s, because the African American population was segregated in certain neighborhoods, mostly "below the hill," certain schools increased the black populations dramatically. Among these schools were Lincoln Elementary, J.B. Young Junior High School, and Central High School. I attended all three of these schools as a child.

With all that said and done, our education was top-notch, our sense of community was strong, and the crime rate was very low because everyone took responsibility for everyone else's child or wayward uncle. Many who were less fortunate than my family would solicit my parents help to be their political voice with the police or with other racial challenges.

Thus, when I arrived in Milwaukee my greatest concern was whether I was going to get a double or triple cheeseburger on my next trip to Henry's Hamburger Stand. Needless to say, I was ill-equipped and naïve when it came to the inner city way of life.

Mother had found an apartment for us in a diverse community with whites, Blacks, and Latinos from lower to middle economic status. Moving from a five-bedroom, two-story dwelling with a private backyard to a two-story apartment building with community bathrooms was unsettling enough. But the lower socioeconomic area we were now living in engendered a sense of culture shock in me and I had to grow up fast.

Mother was immaculate in her housekeeping; but neighboring tenants were apparently less concerned with cleaning, so we sprayed and set Roach trays throughout the apartment. The wooden floors were so worn that she and I went to a hardware store and purchased four gallons of redwood paint and two gallons of wax. Mother was ashamed of our fall from grace but she put on a strong face and made our renovation efforts into a game. We got on our hands and knees with sponges and sponge-painted two coats of redwood paint and two coats of wax, singing all the while. It was amazing how beautiful the finished product looked. Mother was very resourceful, and I felt a sense of efficacy to be able to have such a positive impact on a potentially negative environment.

We were economically challenged at that point in time, but I never knew it. Back then not many Black women would go to the court system to get child support and alimony. Daddy sent me twenty-five dollars whenever he wanted to. In Iowa my mother, by profession, was a respected music teacher; in Milwaukee she took a bus every day to Gimbels Department store to wash dirty dishes in order to make a living for us.

On my first day of middle school in Milwaukee Mother and I rode the city bus across town to an even lower economic community to embark on my new adventure. Mother was tall, beautiful and larger than life to me. I would do anything to please her and she naturally demanded her respect with nothing more than an intense no-nonsense stare. She walked me into the predominantly Black classroom and immediately I heard snickers of laughter and insults directed my way.

"She needs her mama to bring her to school." "Big baby." And on and on.

I looked around the room. No way these students could be in middle school! Some of the girls had huge Dolly Pardon-like breasts. Some of the boys had scars on their faces making them look much older and harder than their tender years. Clearly, the inner city life had robbed them of the child's innocence that I still bore. I was terrified as I watched my mother leave the classroom.

"Have a good day, Deborah," she said as she headed out the door.

Was she kidding? This little girl from Davenport, Iowa was seriously experiencing culture shock in this big city school. The boys looked at me like I was fresh meat. The girls looked at me with envy and hatred because the boys dared to pay the new girl any attention.

The school bell rang at the dismissal of class and I quickly grabbed my belongings and headed for the bus stop. Seven rough and tough girls blocked my exit from the school gate. They cussed at me and bullied me because I dared to be different. I hoped my silence would defuse the situation; but to my chagrin my apparent fear only tantalized my attackers. All of a sudden, all seven hellions started to pummel me. I shrunk into a ball, which protected me from most of the blows.

From out of nowhere, I heard a yelp. One girl's head hit the ground, then another and another. When I peeked up to see what was happening, there stood my knights in shining armor. Four boys from my homeroom class were slugging these girls like men. The girls ran away and two of my heroes walked me to the bus stop and waited with me until I stopped shaking.

When I arrived home, my mother ran to my side; she cleaned my face and skinned knees as she quietly listened to me tell my story. I couldn't wait to see her reaction after hearing how these streetwise villains had attacked her sweet daughter.

However, Mom was raised in St. Louis and had personal knowledge of the laws of the streets. She looked me straight in my eyes and told me, "When you go to school tomorrow, you had better corner the leader of that pack of wolves and beat her to the ground. You don't have to win the fight but if you don't stand up for yourself, those bullies are going to pick on you each and every day."

What the heck? How was I going to beat up the ringleader and leave the school grounds alive? Then Mom gave me even more incentive. She stated that if I didn't confront my attacker she was going to give me a whipping herself. *Life is not fair!* I thought, fighting tears. But I was an obedient child; so the next day at school I waited by the gate for my target. Not a word was spoken. I approached the ringleader and proceeded to righteously kick her butt in front of God and all her friends. Mom was right! After I accomplished this Herculean feat, this girl and I became the best of friends.

Respect is a way of life in the hood. Respect is what those gang members were demanding that December day in 2010 in the parking lot when they murdered my baby. I believe they were misguided, confusing respect with fear. You cannot force someone to respect you, especially through violence. Respect must be earned.

During the earliest years of my life, my mother had been a force to be reckoned with. She only had to look at us and we children obeyed her completely. Like Monique, Mother had a Hollywood air about her. Just gorgeous. She stood by her minister husband, feeding his parishioners, helping to write his sermons, being a role model of the perfect pastor's wife. As the Minister of Music, she provided a welcoming ambience at his church. And she had three children for him. He benefited from her talents if he deserved it or not.

Though she did not learn to play the piano and organ until she was thirty-two years old, she became quite an accomplished pianist. She belonged to a singing group called the Gospel Messengers. They were well known and even cut a record called "Too Close To Heaven."

In addition to establishing a church choir, she encouraged my sisters and I to form our own singing trio called the Tonettes (our last name was Toney). When my stepbrother Wendell would visit in the summers she taught him to play the piano and sing, and he joined us in the group. Ellouise was the soprano, Beatrice was the alto, I was the contralto, and Wendell was the star. We sang gospel music for churches. We became well known in and about the community and even sang at Mother's funeral.

Mother worried that she was forcing music on her children, and with me being the last one she gave me a choice. I could either take piano lessons or play baseball. In view of my love for singing, I regret my childhood choice, but I did learn to play a mean game of baseball.

Music was the center of our life and got our family through many obstacles. We traveled and spent many hours in our car going to church conventions and visiting family members. We would sing all the way. As a child, I remember my favorite song was "I'm A Rolling," which is a spiritual and fit the occasion of traveling down the highways.

Due to racism and our parents' standing in the community, we had a speakeasy in the basement of our house. When famous Black entertainers came to Davenport at times, they would stay with us because the hotels were segregated. Ella Fitzgerald blessed us with her presence in our humble abode. This made Mother happy.

When I reflect on Mother, I think of music and pain. The pain came from my father, Harold. Their relationship was quite dysfunctional. I believe they loved each other, but both had strong personalities that quite frequently clashed. Daddy was a womanizer and cheated on my mother on many occasions. Three outside children were born to my knowledge. My father had his demons and my mother allowed his dysfunctional behavior until she and I left for Milwaukee. When she was on her deathbed, we called Daddy to come to the hospital because this woman with whom he had been married for twenty-one years and who bore him three children was dying. He was with another woman and declined to come saying he did not want to get involved. His insensitivity angered me to the point that I cut his head out of every family picture and did not speak to him for ten years. Yet with all his challenging behaviors, to me he represented strength, possessed a work ethic second to none, and I loved him dearly.

Mother's life was another story about an overcomer. She'd had a tough childhood; her own mother had left her and her brother with their father to be with another man. Instead of hating her, Mom insisted that we travel to Tennessee to pick her up because she had no one. My grandmother lived with us until her death. Mom was my hero for that.

When my mother and I first moved to Milwaukee my oldest sister, Ellouise, was already married with children and my middle sister, Beatrice, was attending college at Iowa State University. My sisters were six and seven years older than me. Mom and I had only lived in Milwaukee for about a year and a half before her cancer dictated our return to Iowa. My Aunt Marcella Hamer—my mother's brother's wife—took us in.

Mother was old school and thought her cancer was something she had to suffer alone. She knew she had it almost five years prior to her death, but my sisters and I had no clue. While her body was racked with pain in the hospital she still would not take pain medication because "it was God's will." Mom died two months after our return from Milwaukee on December 20, 1964. To my mind she died a martyr, though she hated leaving her children behind.

The death of my mother was my first experience with the Black Hole of grief. I was young, angry, disconnected and vowed never to love again because when you love someone they leave you. But I did love. I became a mother in my own right and had three children of my own. Little did I know those feelings of anger, disconnectedness, and emotional isolation would overcome me again, as an adult, when my own life as a mother was shattered by inner city violence.

CHAPTER 2

My First Angel

AFTER MY MOTHER DIED MY Aunt Marcella, who was married to my Uncle Charles, my mother's brother, affectionately took me under her wing and raised me as her own. All of four foot, nine inches tall, she easily weighed a hundred and eighty pounds. My uncle was 6-foot-4, so their interactions were almost comical in nature. I referred to her as "Butterball" because of her physical appearance. But she had a heart of gold.

She was from St. Louis, Missouri, and her marriage to Uncle Charles was her third marriage. She could never bear children so she latched on to me. She would always stand her ground against the gentle oak that was my uncle. Many of their arguments were about me. He thought I should be made to go live with my father and his new family; but she maintained that my wish and my mother's wish was for me to continue living with her where love abounded.

Auntie was way cooler than my parents and most people her age, and permissive to my teenage whims. She would let me go to parties and wear a little make-up. She had few rules, but was very hands-on in knowing and entertaining my friends. I swear they were coming to visit *her* sometimes and not me. Everyone loved and respected Aunt Marcella. She was immersed in the Motown era as my friends and I would imitate being the Supremes, the Temptations, Marvin Gaye, etc.

She was also the social bug because she would have her weekend card parties at the house with my uncle and their friends. She worked as a domestic during part of my teenage years, and I remembered her bringing home leftover food from the rich, white people's parties she served. She was a phenomenal cook—homemade rolls that would melt in your mouth—and eating was one of our greatest pastimes.

Auntie did a wonderful job guiding me through my tumultuous teenage years. In High School I played the violin in the orchestra, and I remember being reprimanded by the conductor because I was being too animated while playing the Messiah. I remember having my first boyfriend; he played on the varsity wrestling team. I remember being so embarrassed because PE was my first class of the day and we were learning to swim. At that time Black Pride was not embraced, and my hair would be so-called Nappy after swimming class, and I would have to endure the teasing from my peers the rest of the day.

I remember one civil rights activity that the high schoolers were involved in an effort to embrace diversity and to integrate the city. We all went out in public with interracial couples that were assigned to us by the group. We had a blast going bowling and eating French fries and watching the sneers of disbelief in the white patrons' eyes. This was our big movement for civil rights. I went on a date with a handsome blond-haired, blue-eyed boy and he was really nice. At the end of the project he took me home and tried to kiss me good night. I told him in no uncertain terms that I would kick his ass if he touched me. So much for tolerance.

During those years, Aunt Marcella was a Godsend. I not only experienced the normal hormonal changes of becoming a teenager during my time with her, but I was a grieving and confused teenager. So, at times Auntie's hands were full trying to deal with my mood swings. She never used a domineering approach in disciplining me. We always talked and I was always the wiser for it.

Auntie was instrumental in helping me to maintain my sanity. I remember one event after mother's death that took place in my Aunt's bathroom. I don't know what the pills were but I took half a bottle in an attempt to kill myself. To my chagrin, I woke up on the bathroom floor and had to face my new realities. I never told Auntie because I wanted her to believe that I had it all together.

There was no way I could repay the love, patience and nurturing Auntie showered on me after my mother's death. All that I am is largely due to her parenting during my teenage years; she provided me with unconditional love at such a difficult time in my young life.

By 1968, my middle sister, Beatrice, had met her first husband, Rodney, and followed them to Chico, California, a small town north of Sacramento. She had always hated Iowa, and didn't want me to be a country bumpkin. She felt I would have a better opportunity for a happier life in California. I was fifteen and in my selfish state I followed my sister out west and left my Aunt Marcella alone. Auntie encouraged it and was supportive of anything that would make me happy. Even if it meant leaving her. I only now know how the loneliness of losing a daughter feels.

Auntie was my first angel. Unfortunately, on September 2, 2007, I lost this angel to congestive heart failure, a genetic condition I was to be challenged with myself a few short years later.

CHAPTER 3

Life's a Mystery

WHENEVER I FIND MYSELF IN a crisis, I resort to writing to alleviate the pain. The occasion of Auntie's death was not any different. To relieve my grief, I put pen to the paper and proceeded to write the following poem in honor of Auntie's Home Going Celebration.

<u>LIFE'S A MYSTERY</u>
(By Deborah Nelson)

It's been said that Life's A Mystery and Death is even stranger.
It cannot be logically explained or controlled.
When it comes to take a loved one away,
Death happens in many mysterious stages.
He appears to be cruel and heartless.
Leaving many grieving souls behind.
There's only one name that can bring comfort
from the void and the pain.
That name is Jesus, who can remove Death's vicious stain.
Not only is Jesus the Comforter but He is the
Righteous Lamb of God.
Who sacrificed His precious blood.
So Death, You have no hold today, tomorrow or forever.
Because All of God's Children will be resurrected,
to behold Jesus face to face.

The Last Portrait: A Psalm For Monique

So yes, you've taken the life of my mother, my auntie,
my friend,
But because of Christ, she is singing, dancing, and shouting
throughout the golden streets of Heaven.

I hear that Jesus sent her some companions to escort her
to her new mansion in the sky.
And she reared up four times in a mighty victorious fashion.
She reared up once for the Holy Ghost and His anointing spirit.
She rose up again for Jesus, and laid her burdens in
His sweet loving arms.
She rose a third time. To greet the Almighty God,
to let all know that He is definitely real!
Then she lifted her fragile body, one last time
to shout to all the demons that by the Grace of God,
She was Free At Last!

My biological mother's headstone reveals a Hebrew scripture.
"Some have entertained Angels unawares."
Who would have believed that in my unworthy lifetime,
That God would send me two Angels
To guide me, to nurture me, to provide unconditional love.
Aunt Marcella.
Little Mama, when my last day finally comes,
will you please calm all of my fears and meet me
at the Heavenly Gate to behold the Son of God?

From earliest childhood I've embraced poetry. I like the flow of it; I like the message of it. One of my major influences in life was Maya Angelou. I love her poetry. I think anytime I go through any stress in life, or through life transitions, I am moved to put it into poetry.

On the very day in 1968 that I moved from Iowa to California, Robert Kennedy was assassinated. The news of that tragedy impacted me so much that I wrote a poem about his death on the airplane. When I arrived in Chico, the little local newspaper published my poem.

My family members, whether on the occasion of their birthdays or deaths or any milestones, all of them have a poem from me. For my son Richard's fortieth birthday I wrote him a poem instead of buying a gift. On Valentine's Day I wrote a poem for my daughter Tamora instead of purchasing her a gift.

Life's Mystery continued for me when just three years after my first angel, my Aunt Marcella, died I was to lose another even more special angel in my life, my dear Monique. Poetry is the way that I express my sorrow, my joy, my life—with one exception: after the most devastating event of my life, I have not been able to find the words to express how penetrating the pain is that I've been experiencing.

I haven't yet been able to write a poem about Monique.

CHAPTER 4

A New Life, A Family of My Own

WHEN I MOVED TO CALIFORNIA in 1968, it was to live with my sister Beatrice and her first husband, Rodney. I was fifteen at the time and Beatrice had convinced me that there was more opportunity to be had out west. She invited me to move in with them, and I did. But I moved out again when I was sixteen. Those were challenging times for me, with the death of my mother still weighing heavily on my heart. I was living on my own and attending night school to achieve my high school diploma. Fortunately, I'd gotten a job working at the Navy recruiting office during the daytime.

Despite the challenges, I actually managed to graduate early from high school and was awarded a scholarship from the Upward Bound Program to attend Chico State College. It was a miracle that I was afforded the opportunity to attend college at all. However, college turned out to be a culture shock of its own making—for the first time I was experiencing social and independent freedom while facing the political and cultural issues that overwhelmed college campuses in the 1970s. And I partied a lot.

I had my first positive experience with the police in Chico. It was during Pioneer Week, which was an extended community party at the college. Police, residents and students all danced and drank in the streets all week long. In college, I also found my social justice voice for civil rights, women's rights, and freedom of expression. And, I met the man who would become the father of my children.

Richard Bernard Nelson and I married in 1970. Immediately afterward I transferred to Sacramento State University to be with him. As a married student, I led a very responsible, boring, collegiate life and graduated in 1973 with a degree in Social Work. Richard and I began banking careers with Bank of America. Three years later, on February 3, 1976, our first child, Richard Anthony Nelson, was born.

The day little Richard was born it snowed in California—an omen on how special this child would be and is. I was twenty-four years old and I had taken proactive steps to insure that his father and I were healthy before conceiving this baby. I had been married for seven years, had a successful career as a banker, and very much wanted this pregnancy.

I was not disappointed. Everything went perfectly according to plan. To induce my labor, I went on a five-mile hike, had a glass of wine, and went immediately into labor when I arrived back home. Two hours later, I delivered a perfect baby boy.

Although I thought he was the greatest thing since sliced bread, his first baby picture revealed a little white wrinkled baby boy weighing 6 pounds 4 ounces. After three months of breast-feeding, this fragile baby blew up to 32 pounds and the doctors were demanding that I focus on having him lose weight. We were so proud of our first born, and he was one of the healthiest and most beautiful babies that our family had ever seen.

He was spoiled rotten, of course, and had intense eyes. One day as a young mother I was home with baby Richard and trying to make him laugh by making a lot of "ga-ga-goo-goo" sounds to amuse him. To my chagrin, he seemed to be annoyed by my immature display and focused an unwavering stare on me that chilled me to the bone. Eventually he came around and smiled, but at that moment I knew he would be a no-nonsense kid. I, on the other hand, was a neurotic, novice mother and rushed him to the emergency room on numerous occasions. I remember reading a book written by the famous pediatrician, Dr. Benjamin Spock, in which he stated that a healthy child needed to have a bowel movement daily. Well, one-day baby Richard did not have the required bowel movement, so I rushed him to the emergency department. The doctors told me I needed to take a chill pill.

Due to our careers with Bank of America, my husband and I vacillated back and forth from Sacramento to Southern California. However, these moves did not hinder us from having two additional dynamic girls. On October 11, 1978 Tamora Rochelle Nelson was born. I delivered her at Panorama City Kaiser Hospital. I had been working at Bank of America in Glendale until my ninth month of pregnancy. It was an easy pregnancy, which correlates with Tamora's easy-going personality. The day I went into labor, I can remember laying on the cold, hard bathroom floor in our home in Northridge, which brought great comfort to me. My husband would periodically come in and check on me as I lay on the floor, until I finally said it was time to go to the hospital. I may have waited a little too long because by time we arrived at the hospital Tamora's head was crowning.

As the nurse came to the car, I told her the baby was coming and I could feel her head outside of my body. Nevertheless, the nurse said it was policy that I had to enter the hospital in a wheelchair. That provoked the most excruciating pain that I experienced during the entire labor process. I can remember that I was quickly wheeled into the labor room and semi-conscience as they undressed me. Within forty minutes my beautiful 6 pounds 7 ounces baby girl was born.

The most profound memory I had during her delivery was when she entered this world. Tamora was screaming her head off. As soon as the doctor placed her in my arms, she looked up into my eyes and immediately stopped crying.

The nurses said, "Oh boy, she knows who her mama is." Tamora and I have been extremely close ever since.

Monique Roxanne Nelson, the last of the Mohicans, was born January 17, 1980 at Kaiser Hospital in Sacramento. I couldn't have been more pleased with her date of birth because January 17th was my childhood hero's birthday—Muhammad Ali.

Monique's birth experience taught me patience and that life does not always go the way I plan. Monique was conceived when I thought I had cervical cancer. After Tamora's birth, I had been informed that the doctors suspected that I had cervical cancer and that within six weeks a hysterectomy would be needed to remove the cancer cells. I was terrified, because I was a new mother with two children under the age of three and diagnosed with the Big C that had been the killer of my mother.

During this six-week waiting period, I did not take any birth control because I knew a hysterectomy was eminent. When I returned to the doctor for the procedure, a couple of tests were taken and he embarrassedly reported to me that an error had been made. Happily, I did not have cancer. However, he said, I was three weeks pregnant. Boy, did I experience a whirlwind of emotions. Shortly after receiving this report, our family relocated to Sacramento where my precious Monique was born with just thirty minutes of labor at an impressive 6 pounds 9 ounces—my largest baby. Monique's birth made our family circle complete.

During those early years, I took the opportunity to stay home with the children. And I learned that life with three children never provides for a dull moment. One Sunday morning when Monique was about two years old, I was busily getting the children ready for church. Richard, who was almost six at that time, had on a three-piece powder blue suit. And I always dressed my girls like twins, this day with pink lace dresses. I let the kids play in the backyard while I, being ever the responsible mother, multitasked by washing dishes and watching them from the kitchen window. We had a swimming pool with a black iron gate around it and I thought the gate was locked. I repeatedly glanced out the window to ensure that the children were safe.

At one point, just as I looked up and out the window, I saw my six-year-old son jump into the swimming pool—with his new church suit on! I was livid, to say the least. He was an accomplished swimmer, even at such a young age, and always swam with a toy in one hand while swimming with the other. But still I quickly rushed out the back door intending to spank his behind for swimming in his new suit.

As I approached the pool, he dove again—this time into the six-foot-deep end of the water. When he resurfaced, low and behold, he was holding his baby sister Monique with one arm and swimming to the edge with the other. I was on the verge of hysteria. I hadn't seen her fall into the pool, and the thought of what could have happened without her big brother being there was paralyzing. In shock, I grabbed both kids from the water.

Richard immediately started teasing his little sister like he always did. "Ha, ha! Monique fell in the pool."

His jesting had a calming effect on Monique and instead of being petrified she started laughing with him. Boy, did we stay on our knees at altar call that Sunday morning! Monique's big brother saved her life when she was a toddler; and he tells me now he wishes daily that he had been with her on December 14, 2010 to try and save her life again.

Monique, especially, was always keeping me on my toes. When she was very young we lived on Bettina Way in Sacramento. She was playing with her brother and sister and in some peculiar way managed to get her head stuck between the black iron gate posts on the edge of the kitchen floor. I tried and tried to free her with no success. Then I started panicking and screaming because I didn't know what to do.

I looked out the front door and saw our friendly mail carrier placing the mail in our box. I ran out of the house screaming at him; he was startled and could not understand a word I was saying. He reluctantly followed me into the house and immediately saw Monique in this strange predicament. He coolly asked me if I had any butter or Crisco. I ran and got both, and he applied the greasy substances around Monique's neck. He tenderly twisted and pulled her upper body until she was freed from her entrapment. Through it all, Monique was courageous; never complained or cried; but of course I was thoroughly annoyed with the whole situation.

When Monique turned five I took a part-time job as a volunteer and instructional aide in the children's school system to stay active and to keep an eye on them. Unfortunately, my marriage wasn't to last. Richard and I divorced in 1986. After my divorce, I found myself as head of the household raising three rambunctious children ranging in age from six-ten years old.

Fortunately for Monique, elementary school provided a wonderful environment for growth. One day she came home from school all excited that she had successfully auditioned to play the Queen of Hearts in the play, *Alice In Wonderland*. She was attending Sequoia Elementary in Sacramento at the time. She asked me to make her costume for this once-in-a-lifetime affair. Having no prior experience as a seamstress, I tried to play the role that I am

Every Woman and that this new task was no problem for me. I went to the local fabric shop and bought a white, soft, fur-like fabric to serve as a regal cape. Then I bought some red ribbon and a red velvet-like material to make the hearts to affix to Her Majesty's cape. In addition, I shopped around until I found a crown that was appropriate for my little queen. It took me two days to complete this project but Monique loved the finished product.

She worked hard to memorize her lines and I had the opportunity to sit in on one of the rehearsals. My friend Anna Hackett's son Sean also was in the play. He played the character of Tweedledee with another schoolmate complementing him as Tweedledum. But the funniest character of all was the little boy who played Monique's husband, the king. Talk about polar opposites!

Monique was always the tallest student in her classroom as her son, Jayden, is today. In the fourth grade, she stood at a statuesque five feet tall. Paul, the young boy playing the king next to my child, seemed somewhat vertically challenged at a mere four feet tall. My Monique had the smoothest ebony skin. Her play husband was white as a sheet. Monique had a loud boisterous voice like her mother's that demanded attention. Her play husband seemed very timid and shy with the softest of high-pitched voices.

When my baby girl would shout, "Off with your head!" the audience would roar.

When Paul would timidly reply, "Yes, Dear," the audience responded with thunderous laughter.

Whoever was responsible for the casting in this production was a visionary. The casting worked; the play was a huge success and raised an impressive amount of money for the school program. The greatest benefit for us was that Monique's first acting experience did wonders in building her self-esteem and encouraged her to know that the sky is the limit with hard work and a positive attitude.

Monique, like Richard and Tamora before her, went on to Albert Einstein Middle School in Sacramento and eventually graduated from Hiram Johnson West Campus High School. However, during those middle school years she was not particularly fond of school.

One morning, in 1991, she woke up and said, "I don't feel well. I can't go to school today."

She had just missed a couple of days of school the prior week and the doctor said he could not find anything wrong with her. I figured that she was just faking it again to get out of going to school. I had to report to work. So what does a domineering mother do? Send her kid to school anyway.

Shortly after I arrived at work, I received a call from the school principal stating that Monique was in the nurse's office again. I explained to him that I had just taken her to the doctor last week and her pediatrician could not find anything wrong with her. He insisted that she was truly complaining about not feeling well and that I should pick her up immediately.

Prior to picking her up, I called and made an urgent care appointment with her pediatrician again. When I picked her up from school she looked flushed and complained of chest pains. Then I started to worry! The pediatrician ran a number of tests this time and discovered that Monique had pleurisy with an enlarged heart. He immediately admitted her to the hospital where two other specialists were contacted to assist with the diagnosis. Monique was prescribed a heavy dose of prednisone to reduce the fluid around her heart.

As my child lay in that hospital bed, I started to suffer an anxiety attack. Why didn't I believe her when she said she didn't feel well? What kind of cruel, negligent mother was I? Aren't mothers supposed to be right at all times?

After a couple of days of testing, the doctors ascertained that Monique was suffering from an autoimmune deficiency disease. Their first diagnosis was leukemia. This news was extremely difficult to digest. Wasn't leukemia a cancer of the blood system? Worse yet, couldn't it be fatal? The doctor sent me home to get some rest as I wrestled with this diagnosis.

I was driving so erratically on my way home that a police officer pulled me over. When he approached the car and asked for my driver's license, the stress from the day overshadowed me and I started crying hysterically. This Godsend of an officer rocked me in his arms as I tried to tell him about my child's illness. Confident that I was not driving under the influence of an illegal substance, this gentle soul of a man escorted me home safely and reassured me that everything would be alright.

I slept little that night and returned to the hospital at the break of dawn. The doctors were performing additional tests because there seemed to be some discrepancy between their original diagnoses. Monique was given a spinal tap, the painful probing and poking with needles of which she underwent in a courageous manner. The new test results determined that my baby did not have leukemia after all. She would be plagued with another autoimmune deficiency disease called lupus.

Lupus is a disease that can damage organs and other parts of the body. Normally our immune system produces antibodies that protect the body from viruses, bacteria, and germs. However, with lupus, something has gone wrong and the immune system can no longer tell the difference between viral and bacterial invaders and the body's healthy tissues, and so the healthy tissues are attacked and destroyed. The result is inflammation, pain, and damage to various organs of the body. Lupus is a chronic disease, tending to go in and out of remission with flare-ups during times of stress. After researching the causes and effects of this disease, I realized it could be equally as life-threatening as leukemia. The worst information was that there was no cure for lupus.

To have a chronic illness as a twelve-year-old adolescent can present many psychological and physical challenges for a child. While Monique's peers were busy playing and attending parties, Monique was being treated for a disease that could alter her way of life and, if it attacked her internal organs, could prove to be fatal. For my baby to have to consider death at such an early age was potentially devastating to her and to us as a family.

However, you have no idea of what kind of fighter my youngest daughter was. She studied this disease and made her mind up not to give it any power over her life. She followed the doctor's instructions and read the literature of how to live with lupus and she kicked lupus' butt! This disease lied dormant in her body for seven years and did not return until she became pregnant with the love of her life, Jayden.

One of my greatest regrets about losing my mother so early in my life was that she would have insured that all three of my kids would've had music lessons. I did the best I could without her direct influence. Richard played the violin in elementary school. Tamora danced. But it was Monique who loved to sing as I do and as my mother had. And Monique had a beautiful voice.

One of her greatest moments was in high school. She was selected to sing the national anthem at a school assembly. Her peers were wowed by her performance of the *Star Spangled Banner* and her self-esteem blossomed. She also sang in school choirs and made a video on YouTube.com singing the Stevie Wonders song *Ribbons in the Sky*. She loved to sing. She would have made her Grandma proud.

As a single parent I faced many challenges, obstacles, and financial issues and had to make many sacrifices to provide for my children. My relations with the children's father were dismal, leaving me with feelings of being alone in this struggle. At times I know the children felt I was too strict and probably way too stressed out. But still, I always considered myself blessed because I never had behavioral problems with the children or drug issues in the family. As small children I kept them in church, but as teenagers it was more of a challenge to keep them going every Sunday. Various childhood rebellions reared their head, especially with Monique. After being diagnosed with lupus, despite her fighting spirit, she rebelled. The medications made her face swell, which negatively impacted her self-esteem. She defied authority, and her inner fear of dying made her take more risks than needed.

For their part, after my divorce my children sacrificed their emotional needs for the greater good of the family. They visited their father every other weekend and seemed to adjust well to their new lifestyle. I sought counseling for them. After interviewing the children, the counselor said that Tamora and Monique blamed themselves for the breakup, believing it was because they had not kept their rooms clean. Self-blaming is considered normal for children during a divorce. However, Richard stated that the reason his parents were divorced was because women do not do what men tell them to do. Needless to say, he had additional sessions with the therapist. The break up was probably hardest on Monique, though, because she was a Daddy's baby.

My children developed very close bonds growing up because, during most of their life, all they had and trusted were each other. They were typical teenagers in search of their purpose in life. In high school Richard was focused on getting ready for college, was bilingual in English and Spanish, played basketball, and was very popular in school. He would always play jokes on his younger sisters, and family was very important to him.

He embraced his role as the Protector. The only time Richard was ever suspended from school was when he was fighting to protect his sister, Tamora, from an aggressive inner-city young man at the high school. I told the Principal that I gladly accepted that suspension because I taught my children to look out for each other. As I mentioned earlier, he literally saved Monique's life. In high school she was assigned a writing assignment on who had had the most influence in her life. Monique wrote about her big brother and how he had been a mentor in her life. Monique and Richard had a unique loving relationship of mutual respect and brotherly and sisterly love.

Tamora was more of a deep thinker as a teenager and often found herself battling depression--hormones kicking in, possibly. More solitary than her siblings, she would worry and desired to become independent and to have her own car and apartment. Yet she ran track, spoke fluent Spanish, and was a genuinely kind person.

Tamora and Monique were confidants and always had each other's back. Although Monique was a lot taller than Tamora during their teenage years, she still was the baby sister.

Monique turned out to be the independent one of the three. She knew no strangers, and was quite gregarious. She had the same Protector-type personality as her brother. Her friends meant a lot to her; she liked to sing and was a member of the drill team at school.

Despite the lupus and the challenges of those turbulent teenage years—or maybe because of them—Monique was becoming a supremely strong black woman, one who would not accept nor desire help from anyone.

CHAPTER 5

We Will Love Our Children Into Excellence

AFTER MY LIFE LESSON IN inner city Milwaukee as a young girl, who would have thought that almost twenty-five years later I would become not only a teacher but also principal of a school that closely resembled my childhood "school of hard knocks?" And who could have thought that very same school would spawn the gang member who became the catalyst in a series of events leading to the shootout, which took my own child's life?

Shortly after my divorce, and while my children were still little, I enrolled in National University to begin my graduate studies. I obtained my teaching credential in 1989 and my Masters of Science and my Instructional Leadership and Administrative credential in 1993.

I chose the field of education not out of desire but out of need. After working in the banking industry for five years and ending a sixteen-year marriage, I suddenly found myself a single parent with no job. While volunteering in my children's classrooms, their teachers started telling me they could see I had a certain knack with children, and they encouraged me to go into teaching. But the cornerstone of my decision to enter the field of education was the local newspapers. The newspapers would randomly and frequently publish articles about the educational failure of children of color and children of poverty in the public school system. The hidden message was that this unique group of students seemed to be unmotivated and were somehow from a lesser intelligence gene pool.

From the very beginning, I knew this hogwash was propaganda and not true. The relentless media coverage reinforced the myth that children of color and children from poverty just cannot learn at high levels like their white counterparts. There seemed to be no level playing field taking place in public schools within urban America.

As a pastor's daughter, my sisters and I were raised to be the voice of and to embrace the cause for the underdog. Life experiences had more than adequately prepared me to champion the cause for at-risk students in the public school system. Reading about and experiencing the many injustices that still exist for people of color in this society, especially in the public school system, motivated me to get involved. With this sense of injustice burning within my soul, I embarked on a professional career as an educator with a passion to make a noted difference. I worked my way up from a three-hour instructional aide to a classroom teacher to an elementary school principal.

Richard, Tamora, and Monique were teenagers by this time and my greatest helpmates in taking care of themselves and me while I attended school at night and worked during the day. Many, many times I wanted to give up the fight but my cherubs would not allow it.

In retrospect, many of their needs went unmet while I was trying to attain a profession to support them and guide them toward their college education. We had family meetings where they inspired me to continue my professional goals and vetted their complaints about my parenting. Many times I did not attend *their* parent/teacher conferences because I was conducting parent conferences for my students. The three of them seemed to be truly proud of me. They supported our family the best they could, even sharing the cooking. However, in retrospect, I would certainly do it differently by spending all the time in the world with my children. Too bad life is not a dress rehearsal.

In 1995 I landed my first principalship at David Lubin Elementary School in East Sacramento, where I learned the ins and outs of the haves and the have-nots in public education. A higher socio-economic community, the average parent in that school held a master's degree and maintained a six-figure salary with various state and federal government positions. The resources and levels of involvement of this predominately white community were quite impressive and came with a variety of rewards and sanctions. Although I was their first encounter with a person of color as a principal, I must say those seven years provided me with an invaluable experience in education.

I left David Lubin Elementary when the school year ended in 2000 to serve at the district office as a Principal on Special Assignment. There I had the opportunity to do research on effective programs for African-American youth and to collect information on successful models throughout the nation.

My next challenge as an educator would take that research and put it into practice. I was offered the opportunity to take on the leadership of Parkway Elementary School, one of Sacramento's inner city schools.

When I started at Parkway in August of 2001 it was the lowest achieving school in a district of 55,000 students; it had been identified by the State of California as a "Program Improvement School." Meaning that it had nowhere to go but up. Approximately seventy percent of the student body was of African-American descent. Thirty percent were English Language Learners. One hundred percent of the student population participated in the free and reduced lunch program.

The majority of the student body that we served at Parkway lived in a lower socio-economic community called Franklin Villa. At that time, "the G," as the neighborhood was often referred to, had the highest violence, drug abuse, and child molestation rates in Sacramento County. Many families exhibited a sense of hopelessness due to the detrimental cycle of generational poverty and generational educational failure in the public school system. Some naysayers said that this was the formula for disaster as far as Parkway was concerned; but I believed God had another plan. Though how that plan was to be achieved was yet to be determined.

My first day as principal at Parkway Elementary School I had to call a SWAT team out. This was just sixty minutes after the first bell rang. An employee and a parent were feverishly fighting, ranting, and raving throughout the school campus because of something said to the son of the parent. Suddenly, someone screamed, "Gun!" and the police were called. After their investigation, the persons engaged in the altercation were cited and removed from the campus. Forty minutes later, I received a 911 call from a classroom where a fourth grade student was assaulting the teacher.

Shortly after the school year started, I was called to report, in person, to the Board of Education and present my "Plan of Action" as to how I was going to rectify the situation at Parkway—both academic and behavioral. Nervous in front of this esteemed group of power-brokers, I nevertheless proceeded with the details of how I planned to accelerate the rate of student achievement: having a relentless focus on instruction, using only researched-based strategies, building a professional learning community where all could thrive, collaborating with all stakeholders, establishing a data-driven culture, and hiring and maintaining quality staff members. In my closing comments, I confidently stated, "If all the foregoing measures fail, then we will simply love our children into excellence." The room erupted into laughter; but this statement would be our mantra and the cornerstone of our vision for the next seven years at Parkway Elementary School.

While all evidence pointed to the need to overhaul every component of the school—the instructional program, day to day operations, the organizational structure, school climate, school safety, external and internal programs—my immediate focus became the staff.

It was clear the teachers' focus was on the bad behavior and the dysfunctional family backgrounds of the students, not on instruction. The staff lounge had become an extremely toxic environment. "Those kids can't learn." "Those kids act like animals." "You know his mama is a crack head." "Those kids cannot be successful coming from that kind of environment." And on and on and on. The number one sport of the staff seemed to be to blame the victims for the state of educational and social failure at the school.

I couldn't wait until *those* kids became *our* kids.

The demographics of the school were such that the majority of the students were African Americans from families living in poverty. The staff was largely white and middle class. My first impression was that they seemed to be afraid and culturally disconnected from the student body they served. Many of the Parkway teachers' fears had turn into total dislike of the students. Compounding that, because these students consistently failed, the teachers were considered failures as educators. So instead of taking responsibility for teaching and learning, or taking responsibility for student behaviors, their tactic was to blame the children. The question that was keeping me awake at night was: how is an outspoken black female principal going to get buy-in from a white staff that fostered a belief system totally contrary to the very fiber of her being? Nevertheless, for the sake of the children, I had to try.

My first stratagem was to work with a committee of teachers to condense the rules—pages and pages of *thou shalt nots*—to three main rules that could be expanded: 1) Be Safe; 2) Respect Yourself and Others; and 3) Follow All Adult Instructions. Once the school rules had been clarified and drafted into positive statements, the Leadership Team turned its attention to executing the Schoolwide Discipline Plan in an efficacious manner. Of course, as the school principal I could have just presented the plan at a staff meeting and it would have been quick and easy. It would have also been totally ineffective. The goal was for the teachers to take their school back. The only way this feat could be achieved was if they took total responsibility for student behaviors not just in their classroom but for *every* student throughout the campus.

The Leadership Team presented the Schoolwide Discipline Plan to the school community. It was communicated to the parents in a newsletter and reinforced to students in a schoolwide assembly once a trimester. Additional strategies to create a positive learning environment were enacted, including teaching the *Second Step* anti-violence curriculum in the classroom, practicing rules and procedures on a regular basis, holding students and teachers accountable for the plan, and providing a weekly positive incentive program to motivate students to do the right thing.

Except for a couple of extreme behavior problems that had to be handled at the administrative level, the students at Parkway responded positively to the high standards and clear expectations for day-to-day operations.

My next job was to beef up the academic portion of the students' day. I instituted a school-wide focus on reading and literacy, provided professional development opportunities to introduce more effective instructional strategies, and implemented an extended day program to provide students access to performing arts, organized sports, hands-on experiences in science, and tutoring. The extended day programs provided the added benefit of being a safe haven for students after school hours.

I also reached out to our community business partners to recognize and honor the students' individual and collective efforts by donating rewards such as gift cards, savings bonds, and field trips. Local stores provided enrichment grants to expose our students to the arts and the science curriculum. They also provided volunteers and mentors so our scholars could see that their education did not take place in a vacuum but was supported and embraced by the entire community.

The local NBA team, the Sacramento Kings, adopted us for the entire year providing Parkway a computer learning center fit for a King, literature books, field trips to their games, campus visits, and inspirational assemblies with plenty of media coverage. They truly made a difference in enhancing our educational program in a neighborhood that was not embraced by the status quo

In 2001, the Parkway students that I first observed were little people with hallow eyes who had been robbed of their childhoods. Most of the discipline problems and altercations that took place were due to children who, for their survival, had to act like adults. Unfortunately, many of them did not have a quality adult in their life to emulate. Therefore, acting like dysfunctional adults was more the norm. Violence was a daily factor that hovered in their communities and in their homes. Infractions in school ranged from rebelling against authority to smoking marijuana in the bathrooms—and this was a K-6 school!

Mondays were always challenging days for us because someone's parent, relative, or friend had been shot or assaulted over the weekend. Violence, even death, was a common weekend occurrence in the neighborhood my students lived in. The uncanny part for me was how chillingly indifferent the children seemed when death touched their young lives. Violence was so routine in this gated community (which was renamed from Franklin Villa to Phoenix Park after redevelopment in 2004) they had their own satellite police station. We used to wonder if the gates were to keep the residents in or to keep others out.

One Monday, Jacob, a tall "I-can-take-care-of-myself" African-American sixth grader was sent to my office for using obscenities and disrespecting the teacher. Honestly, I never looked forward to disciplining Jacob because you never knew when his fuse would blow. After a short conversation with him, I could ascertain that Jacob's anger had nothing to do with the classroom teacher. I delicately questioned him further about what was *really* troubling him.

This gigantic child, who was well-feared on the playground, proceeded to break down and cry uncontrollably. I gently rocked him in my arms and waited for him to talk in his own time, in his own way. Finally, he blurted out, "I just can't take hearing the bullets being shot past my bedroom every night." He couldn't sleep in fear that one day one of those stray bullets would lodge in his head and end his young life. Yet, we as educators expected him to ignore the atrocities in his life, come to school, follow the rules, and learn at high levels daily. It is not a level playing field in education for the have-nots.

During that first year at Parkway, a superintendent-appointed task force, composed of community members, educators, parishioners, and professionals, described our Parkway Scholars as children who suffer from post-traumatic stress syndrome, much like the children who were victims in the Iraqi War. Their ability to learn was negatively impacted by the residue of poverty and the violent living conditions that they were subjected to.

This was a pretty grim report; but to me these young students desperately needed to become children again. They needed a safe haven, a place that was structured with a daily schedule they could count on. They needed a sense of family and positive reinforcement that would build their self-worth and sense of efficacy. That, I vowed, was what the vision of Parkway Elementary School would become for them.

One of my strategies was to become as visible to the children as possible. Before school, after school I was there connecting with children. During recess, at lunch break I would play racket ball with them and be available to talk about whatever they wished. How do you reverse the negative messages that have been brainwashed into their young minds? By using reverse psychology.

Daily I would walk groups of students home telling them that they were special. They were unique. They were the smartest kids in town. The thing about this technique was that after a hundred and eighty days a year for eight years, the children came to *believe* it.

Then I started meeting with children individually and in groups to share their curriculum-embedded assessments and standardized testing results. Many times in an educational reform movement, the adults host a multitude of meetings on student achievement but rarely do they include the dominant factor in the scenario of academic excellence—the students.

This strategy of letting the students see their test results was extremely effective in setting goals and empowering students to have a voice in the direction of their education. Let's face the facts—you cannot force anyone to learn. Students must have a buy-in to the process and they have to see how a good education can benefit them. Evidence of the effectiveness of empowering students presented itself each summer when I returned to work in August; my office would be full of students—not teachers, not parents—but students wanting to know their results on the state Standardized Testing and Reporting (STAR) testing. When education is important to the child, then we as educators can truly be facilitators of learning. If the value of education was not effectively being communicated in the homes of the Parkway students, then my staff and I would do it double or triple time if we had to, within the six hours the children were under our tutelage.

Slowly but surely, the school—students and staff included—was turning itself around; and the results were showing up on our state standardized test scores. In 2003, Parkway's composite school student achievement score improved by 65 points. The next year it improved by another 55 points. And by 2006 the composite score had improved by yet another 36 points, resulting in a milestone accomplishment of exiting from "Program Improvement" status. In my last year at Parkway, 2007/2008, the composite score improved by yet another ten points. That year Parkway Elementary was recognized as an Honorable Mention School for the Title 1 Academic Achievement Award presented by the California State Department of Education.

I was thrilled in 2006 to be personally honored by the National Coalition of 100 Black Women, Inc. for my work at Parkway; I was given the Education Advocate Award. The event was held at the Double Tree Hotel in Sacramento, and I was so excited that I rushed to the beauty shop, the manicurist, and my favorite boutique to purchase the best fitting pantsuit I could find. My family and my closest friends were invited to be in my *Amen* corner and to share in this prestigious celebration.

There were four other women being honored that day in the areas of Business, Spiritual Leadership, and Living Legend Awards. These women were all well known in the community and I felt that their accomplishments far surpassed the ministry that I was doing at the school. But when your peers to want to acknowledge your efforts, it is such an honor and privilege to experience it. As my mother used to say, "Let me smell my roses while I am still alive." And smelling my roses I certainly did that day. Friends had sent me three dozen of the longest stemmed, blood red, and most gorgeous roses that I have ever seen. For my award, I was given a lovely, inscribed glass statuette.

The sacrifices that we choose to make in life are personal choices. No one makes us do them. It is no secret that the daily challenges that take place in public education require a certain level of sacrifice from all who work there. One of the sacrifices for me had to do with the death of Aunt Marcella in 2007.

During the later years of her life, she had resided in the Davenport Lutheran Nursing Home. She was one of the most popular residents there, primarily due to her heart-warming personality and mesmerizing smile.

Residing three thousand miles apart limited the number of times she and I were able to see each other over the years, but it didn't limit the love. We talked to each other just about every other day, depending on what was going on in our lives.

Auntie's health had been deteriorating for some time. She had acquired congestive heart failure (not genetically related to mine, since we were related by marriage, not by blood); and I frequently could detect that she was laboring to breath during our telephone conversations. My sister, Ellouise, was at Auntie's bedside daily and would call me on a regular basis to share the doctor's report.

The fluid in her lungs was at a dangerous level, I was told. The medical staff would aspirate a liter of fluid from each lung; as the fluid was removed, her lungs would quickly refill. As Auntie's body was beginning to shut down,

I was preparing to open up the 2007/2008 school year at Parkway. Our staff retreat was scheduled and a host of other issues filled my plate. I repeatedly told Auntie, "I'll be home to take care of you as soon as I've open the school doors on September 3rd." She always supported whatever decision I made and was so very proud that her niece was a school principal. She would affectionately say, "Don't worry, Baby. I will be right here until you come home."

On September 2nd, Ellouise called and said, "You better talk to Auntie." The sense of urgency in her voice scared me. I talked to Auntie and begged her to hold on until I got home. My emotions overflowed into a pool of tears and in Auntie's most private moment, instead of thinking of herself, once again, she was comforting me.

As soon as I hung up, I made a bee-hive to the airport without a care about my professional or personal obligations in Sacramento. The first stop was in Denver, Colorado. I desperately called Auntie to reassure her that I would be there within the next four hours. But Ellouise answered the phone. "I'm sorry, Deborah. You're too late." Crying and yelling frantically at the airport, I frightened many of the people who were waiting for the connecting flight. My speech was inaudible and I couldn't stop crying and shaking. Once aboard the plane destined for Iowa, I proceeded with my now lonely trip. Instead of going to comfort my sick aunt, I was continuing this journey to bury the woman who'd served as my mother.

On the plane, a kind-hearted stewardess could see the mental anguish that I was going through. I was heavily grieving and feeling remorseful feelings of guilt. I should have dropped everything and run to her side, I thought. The stewardess brought me a drink, didn't say a word, but just rocked me in her arms. I continued to cry quietly and thanked her immensely for her tenderness.

The sacrifice I made in September 2007 to open up Parkway Elementary School before going to my dying Auntie's side was more than I bargained for. I didn't think I could ever forgive myself. But then again, being a principal continually meant making sacrifices on behalf of my students.

Another kind of sacrifice involved the level of emotional commitment I made to my Parkway families. When our students experienced tragedy—and many did—it was my job as principal to notify the other parents, request school emergency teams to provide counseling for any student having adverse reactions, and to authorize instructional time for school-wide art projects to express condolences for the victim and the victim's family. Ironically, it seemed that the students needing the most support were traumatized not necessarily from the death of a schoolmate but because the situation resurrected memories of past hurts and deaths in their lives. I also felt it was important to support my Parkway families by attending their funerals.

The most moving funeral I attended did not involve gun violence, but for a student who had been run over by a van. Eddie was a sixth grader. I had watched him grow from an awkward third grader into a handsome young preteen. He was unusually bright; he was mischievous but a very kind-hearted child. My last encounter with him was at the school carnival a week prior to his death. I remember thinking. "What a handsome young man he will become one day." And on cue he offered an act of kindness by helping to clean up the school grounds after the carnival. He was on his faithful bicycle and safely returned home after the event.

About a week later, I received a call in the front office that there had been a terrible accident involving Eddie. After visiting friends, Eddie was bicycling home when he was hit by a large van driven by an unlicensed driver. I was told that he'd been oddly trapped beneath the van with his bicycle, and unfortunately was still conscious. Friends tried to talk to him and comfort him as he was suffering under this vehicle desperately waiting for the ambulance to arrive. The following morning at work, when I heard of Eddie's accident, I immediately jumped in my car and rushed over to the hospital to support the family. I was enroute when my secretary called me and shared that the family wanted to be alone at this time because Eddie was in serious condition. Respecting their wishes, I returned to campus. A short time later I received another call telling me that Eddie had died.

The most shocking experience was when I went to the funeral home to pay my respects to the family and to view Eddie's body. His death was so violent and he suffered so tremendously that I did not recognize his body. His color had blackened and the head injury was so severe that a toupee was placed on his head. That handsome face had been mangled beyond recognition. I felt traumatized by what I was witnessing, and I empathized tremendously with the unyielding pain that his family was experiencing.

I was asked by the family to speak on behalf of the Parkway school community at Eddie's funeral. A day or so prior, I had made a home visit to Phoenix Park where his mother and baby sister resided. The traditional niceties and words of condolences were exchanged and the family put on that show of strength expected in the Black Family. But the longer than normal embraces told the true story of their overwhelming pain. At the funeral, I tried to be upbeat and supportive to the family. But inside I was nervous and truly wanted to scream at this heart-wrenching loss. Children dying is an aberration! The theme of my speech was about life not being measured by the number of breaths we take, but by the moments that take our breath away.

The next funeral I attended was the last one before burying my own child. It was for one of the Hmong students at Parkway. Lily, too, was a sixth grader who had contributed to the high achieving student model now established at Parkway. She took to standardized testing like a duck to water and was our Spelling Bee champion at our annual Academic Conference. Lily stands out in my mind because when she was awarded a brand new bicycle for winning the Spelling Bee, she returned it to me. Lily stated that it was enough for her to know she had accomplished this challenging feat. I was blown away by this example of the desire for extrinsic rewards transformed into intrinsic values.

Besides being an exemplary student, Lily was the pride and joy of her family. However, she was often in the front office complaining of stomach pains and we would call her parents to pick her up. One night while she was at home, Lily went into the bathroom and was discovered there the next morning, dead from some mysterious stomach disease at the tender age of twelve. The Hmong culture had several memorial services for Lily that lasted an entire week. Her family openly agonized over their beautiful young angel's death.

At her funeral, I remember talking with her father who had to put on the front of a strong father for the entire Hmong community while secretly inside,

I'm sure, he was ready to explode at the loss of his little girl. Her mother and grandmother openly cried, "Why?!" In step with the Hmong tradition, I took the shovel and threw dirt on Lily's grave in a final good-bye. Just heart wrenching!

Sadly, the most violent deaths and funeral in my entire career happened when I was still at David Lubin Elementary School. A gorgeous biracial couple had the most precious, big-eyed boys in preschool and kindergarten. The mother was the breadwinner; the father was on disability and performed his duties as Mr. Mom, bringing the children to and from school regularly. As fate would have it, the parents' relationship soured and the mother made the decision for the couple to divorce. The father could not bear another failure in his life and did the most horrific act ever. One day after school, in his home in front of his frightened wife, he put a gun to the children's heads and shot them, killing these gorgeous innocent babies instantly. Then he turned the gun on himself. His motive was accomplished in destroying his wife and leaving an indelible mark of destruction on her mind and soul forever. That funeral was beyond words. Two precious little white caskets with bears and balloons attended by a visibly shaken and broken mother to send her children on their way-too-premature Home Going. Can we really call it a "celebration" of their young lives? I think not! Just another demonic domestic violence situation that left a number of victims in its path forever.

The point of recounting these tragic funerals is to illustrate how emotionally involved I became with the school communities in which I worked and which I was charged to lead. That involvement was by design. In order to serve my students and to raise them up academically, I had to give my all to them socially and emotionally.

My own three children were sheltered from the trauma, the violence, the kind of lives my Parkway students were exposed to. *My* family was financially stable at that time and considered to be middle class. Richard, Tamora, and Monique went to Sacramento public schools, but theirs were not in the inner city. I did have to get their teachers straight once in a while at Sequoia Elementary because most of the children of color were also children of poverty and were bussed into the school. Many times, their teachers would just stereotypically assume that my children did not live in the neighborhood but were bussed in.

Even though theirs wasn't an inner city school, Richard, Tamora, and Monique *were* exposed to children from every socioeconomic background at public school. I had taught them that the only reason we were not poor was through the grace of God and to never look down on someone who may be less fortunate. They knew to treat a child from a gang-banger background with the same respect as someone from our neighborhood. Being exposed to more violent neighborhoods was part of my profession. Therefore, my children had no fear of the children from "across the tracks," so to speak. Maybe if they had been afraid, Monique would still be with us today.

The irony of this story is that the very community I had sacrificed for, worked for, and prayed for professionally and on a personal level was the one responsible for taking the most precious commodity from my life—*my* child. This paradox I will never understand.

CHAPTER 6

A New Member of the Family

IN 2007, THE MOST REMARKABLE thing happened. My baby announced she was having a baby! Monique came into this world on January 17, 1980 at Kaiser Permanente hospital in Sacramento. She weighed six pounds, four ounces at birth and was twenty-one inches long. Her baby boy, Jayden, made his arrival at the same hospital twenty-eight years later, on June 2, 2008. Just like his mother, little Jayden weighed in at six pounds, four ounces and measured twenty-one inches long. And just like his mother, baby Jayden looked like his grandfather, my ex-husband, Richard.

Monique had grown to be an exotic beauty. She was the tallest of all of my children at a statuesque five feet, ten inches and full-figured like I was at her age. Monique's eyes were large and gorgeous with a smile to die for. She was exceptionally photogenic with an air of Hollywood about her. She could change her appearance with a new wig or outfit in a minute. We used to always tease her about looking like Queen Latifah, only prettier. But you didn't dare let the physical attractiveness of this woman fool you; she was tough as nails! Monique consistently took up for family members and friends and would fight at the drop of a hat. If you were on her wrong side, beware! If she loved you, it was unconditional.

She had many nicknames, like *MoMo, Big Roxxy*, and *Nicki*. And she had two tattoos that she received at the young age of sixteen and managed to hide from me for a whole year. One said, "Daddy's Girl" and trust me, she was a daddy's girl. The other one was on her hand in italicized writing that simply identified her as *"Monique."*

The doctors had adamantly discouraged Monique from bearing a child because of the lupus, a condition that could be exacerbated by the stress of pregnancy; but she adamantly ignored their advice. Her burning desire to become a mother outweighed any threat to her own life to have a child.

Monique was determined and well-disciplined throughout her pregnancy. Moderate exercise and avoiding fast food became parts of her daily regimen. The doctor appointments were twice as many as for a woman with a typical pregnancy due to her illness. Her lupus specialist frequently monitored her blood levels as a preventative measure to handle any flare-ups she might experience. While she lost weight during the early stages of her pregnancy, that mother's glow so common with pregnant women radiated from her beautiful face, and she exuded with pure joy at the thought of becoming a mother.

Her best friend, Alethea, announced that she was also pregnant, and the two of them were beyond ecstatic at the prospect of both of them having baby boys. I am not certain how they focused on naming their sons with names beginning with J, but they did. Monique selected "Jayden" for her forthcoming cherub and Alethea selected "Jayce."

A month prior to Jayden's arrival, Tamora and I hosted a baby shower for Monique. We purchased a baby crib from Goore's in Sacramento (a popular baby furniture store that has since closed). Approximately twenty friends and family members attended the shower. I was probably more excited than Monique, especially concerning how far she had come with a successful pregnancy. Monique was glowing, the cameras were clicking, and the anticipation of a new family member coming on the scene soon was nothing but bliss. The shower exceeded all expectations and Jayden was going to be well equipped upon his arrival with all the wonderful gifts that were given. Monique repeatedly expressed her appreciation for the baby shower. She wasn't one to accept help or gifts easily. But in celebration of Jayden's birth, she smiled frequently and took the day's activities in fashionable stride.

Once the baby's nest was in order, we enthusiastically awaited the birth of my second grandson. Naturally, I was visibly nervous while supporting Monique throughout this pregnancy. On the one hand, I was happy about the baby; but on the other, I was extremely concerned about Monique's health.

We finally could exhale when Monique successfully completed her first trimester with few complications. She was so excited and thrilled to see her first sonogram. To witness this breathing, thriving human being inside of her was just short of a miracle. Early on, however, Monique had mixed emotions when it came to knowing the sex of her baby. One minute, she wanted to wait and be surprised when the baby was born. The next minute, she would say, "I have to know right now" whether the child was a girl or a boy. Eventually, "right now" won. A boy it would be.

During the ninth month of her pregnancy, I took Monique to the emergency room three times. Her blood tests revealed a flare-up of the lupus due to all the new stressors placed on her physically and emotionally.

On June 1st Monique called me. "Mama, I think my labor has started. I'm feeling contractions and I'm having trouble breathing. I think I need to go to the hospital."

I drove her there immediately. The baby's vital signs were closely monitored, revealing that he was in stress, also. The doctors were worried that the umbilical cord might possibly be wrapped around his throat causing the sporadic and dropping heartbeats. Monique and I watched that monitor like white on rice. Every time the baby's heartbeat took a dive or even stopped, we screamed for the nurse to do something. But the contractions stopped, and the baby's heartbeat returned to normal. So she was eventually sent home.

Vividly, I remember how strong and take-charge Monique was during these three false alarms, and how she always seemed more concerned about Jayden's and my welfare than her own. After that third visit to the emergency room, I took her back to her apartment. "If you need me at any time of the day, just give me a call," I told her.

A little after midnight that same evening, I received a telephone call from Kaiser Permanente hospital stating that Monique had been readmitted into the hospital. *What the heck?* I had explicitly told her to call me when the pain reappeared. But my baby was so stubborn and independent she drove herself to the hospital to have her baby. I probably broke every speeding and red light violation possible as I sped to Kaiser hospital.

Wide-eyed and breathless, I ran into the delivery room shouting, "Where is my child?"

A very patient nurse escorted me to the waiting room and informed me that my daughter was in surgery having a caesarean section. I frantically explained that I was her birthing coach and needed to be in surgery with her. To no avail. The surgery was already in progress and I could not go in to share this remarkable moment with her.

The wait was excruciating. The nursing personnel were compassionate and checked on me frequently. They even provided me with my own private waiting room with the baby's first bottle waiting beside his crib.

Then that momentous time arrived! The nurse walked into the room with this tiny human being in her arms swaddled in a white blanket. She gingerly placed this little bundle of joy in my arms with the bottle of formula. I placed the nipple of the bottle on his lips and Jayden drank for the first time in Grandma's arms.

There are no words to express the mixture of emotions I was experiencing. Memories of holding my own children for the first time flooded my mind: the amazement, love and wonder of looking into their little eyes; counting their tiny toes and fingers; and smelling their pure baby breath. All these heavenly feelings could in no way compare with the feelings I experienced with my grandchild. I know it sounds strange but the exponential love I have for my grandchildren is priceless. It's spiritual, it's jubilant, and they are my legacy. Jayden was perfect from the start. No crying, no fussing, just loving.

Then Monique was rolled into the waiting room, wide-awake, her skin glowing. She was talking nonstop on her cell phone, informing the whole world about her greatest accomplishment, birthing Jayden Anthony Butler-Nelson. Her smile stretched from one dimple to the next. Quite honestly, I had never ever seen her so happy before in my life. Everything was perfect!

After observing Monique's behavior for a few moments, I ascertained that, yes, she was indeed happy—who wouldn't be? However, I realized, the drugs that had been given to her during the surgery were still in her system.

She was almost comical in her euphoria. But alas, the following day her feet were on the ground again. She began feeling the pain from the surgery while addressing the challenges faced with nursing and caring for a newborn baby. The entire family and numerous friends came to visit. Even Jayden's father, Kenyatta Butler, came to visit and share in this gala event. The Kodak moments were many and everything was right with the world.

Monique and Jayden spent the first two weeks at home with me. Although I had raised three children thirty-four years prior, taking care of baby Jayden was like the first time all over again. The anxiety immediately set in because I wanted everything to go smoothly and perfectly in an imperfect world. Monique and I equally overreacted at every little cough, fart, and any irregularities in feeding Jayden. In hindsight, that was the best two weeks of my life.

Monique was the "Guru of Motherhood"—self-sacrificing to a fault and totally head over heels in love with her baby. As she expressed it, all she could "hear, touch, smell, feel and taste" was Jayden Anthony Butler-Nelson. Every void that she'd felt in life, she told me, was immediately filled whenever she looked into Jayden's big brown eyes: love, self-gratification and joy.

To add to her delight, three months after Jayden was born Monique's friend Alethea gave birth to her baby, Jayce. The two boys would spend their first years in each other's company like brothers. Monique regarded Jayce as her "second son."

As baby Jayden grew, Monique confided in me that her favorite time of the day had become early morning. Jayden would pull himself up in his crib, which was located right next to her bed, and softly call her and talk to her until she would awaken. That little voice was music to her ears and became very precious moments for the new mother.

I called Jayden our little Mandingo warrior. He was a typical one-year-old who was very bright and got into everything. Mercy me, don't let that baby fall and hurt himself! It would take minutes to calm his mother down, while in the meantime Jayden would inquisitively crawl on to his next adventure.

Monique made certain that he only ate healthy foods and was extremely responsible that all doctor appointments were done in a timely fashion. Before going to the doctor, she would research any symptoms he might be exhibiting and wrote her focus questions down prior to the appointment.

He completed my daughter and gave her life a sense of purpose. All of her conversations, shopping sprees, present or future plans were centered on Jayden Anthony Butler-Nelson. Her daily telephone calls, text messages, and Facebook comments were about Jayden Anthony Butler-Nelson. To watch the interaction between those two was a sight to behold and nothing but the "Miracle of Love!" Monique was an outstanding mother and showered little Jayden with unconditional love.

Prior to getting pregnant, Monique had been known for being the life of the party. But when little Jayden arrived on the scene, the desire to party faded. I would have to nag her to go out, spend time with her friends and relax! Secretly, I just wanted more time to babysit and spoil that little boy to death. It never failed. She would go out, but then she would return within about forty-five minutes, saying there was nothing out there for her anymore. My baby had grown up to be an exceptional mother.

Throughout that first year, Monique frequently took baby Jayden to the one-hour photo shop on Florin Road to have mother and son photos taken. Both of them are unusually photogenic and complimented each other beautifully in each and every photo they had taken. When she brought the first one home, I would look at that 8x10 portrait and jump ahead in my mind to what that picture might look like when Jayden was five, ten, and even into adulthood. Heart wrenchingly, the trip to the one-hour photo shop in 2010 would prevent any future photo opportunities for Jayden and Monique.

CHAPTER 7

A Carousel of Changes

WHEN I WAS STILL AT the Sacramento City Unified School District office on special assignment, one of my projects was to build a school-community partnership with the California Musical Theatre (CMT), which was sponsored by Wells Fargo Bank. My mission was to build up the arts in the Sacramento schools, because so much of the budget had been cut and all the arts were gone—and that's what kept many kids in school.

While I was campaigning to get sponsorships for district artistic endeavors, one of the CMT representatives challenged me by saying, "Well, if you are really advocating for the arts, what kind of role model are you for the students? You need to perform so you can walk the talk!" Performing with my siblings was something I had enjoyed in my youth; so, in September of 2000 I auditioned for a part in a CMT-sponsored musical called *Gospel at Colonus*.

Written by Lee Breuer (with music by Bob Telson), this mash-up between a classical Greek drama and a Pentecostal gospel rendition offers a musical retelling of Sophocles' tale of Oedipus' redemption. It was quite an ambitious undertaking. All the self-esteem-building that I had tried to instill in my students, such as believing in oneself, taking risks, and exploring new possibilities, seemed more than a little intimidating to me as I faced this challenge. After the audition, I miraculously made the cut and was selected to be a cast member of this dynamic musical. To my delight, I was offered the opportunity to sing the opening solo. I also participated in the Ismene Quartet, whose harmony (if I say so myself) was a splendid piece of art. Our performance was scheduled to be part of the annual Martin Luther King, Jr. Day celebration at the California State University Theater,

To my surprise, one of the others auditioning was Jarvis, a boy who had been a student at David Lubin Elementary School while I was still principal there. His father was a Jamaican musician, and his step-mother was Caucasian and a nurse at one of the local hospitals. Jarvis himself had been born in Jamaica. I will never forget this amazing boy's face and personality. And what a delight to perform with him! We sang and danced together in the musical's ensemble. I vividly remember, during the intermission of one of the performances Jarvis proudly taking my hand and leading me through the mingling audience declaring, "This is my principal!" That was a moment to behold.

The experience of participating in community theatre was so infectious that over the next five years I appeared in twelve additional musicals, including *Evangelize, Hallelujah,* and multiple performances of *Legacy*. The *Legacy* performances were under the direction of Images Theatre founder Lisa Lacy, and held at CSUS's University Theatre. We also performed at a local community theater and even once at the Wells Fargo Pavilion in Sacramento. Performing on stage gave me an incredible amount of balance in my life. I learned that we are so much more than our jobs. Just being able to sing, to be free, and to feel good being around positive people raised up my spirits.

Monique, along with Richard and Tamora, always came out to support me in my musical endeavors. Their continuous support kept me motivated as usual. It's strange how much a parent works for their child's approval as much as the child yearns for their parent's praise and approval.

But I was mainly doing it for the kids. At Parkway, while I was principal, we would organize annual field trips in honor of Martin Luther King, Jr. Day to the *Legacy* productions as enrichment for our Black History curriculum. Written by Lisa Lacy, *Legacy* was a cleverly articulated, yet spiritual synopsis of the Black Experience in America from slavery up until the election of the first African-American president, Barack Obama. I performed a high-spirited, riveting solo called "Freedom," composed by a musical genius named Charles Cooper. I delighted in the feedback I received from my school staff who marveled at my ability to sing and perform. Little did they know that I was the daughter of a preacher and a church musical director, and that performing before an audience came as second nature to me.

Many of the Parkway students and their families attended the Legacy musical productions. The performances were moving, coupled with the emotional impact of being a story of true events. People always left the theater in tears; it had such an impact. But it had more of an impact on the people who participated in it, particularly the children. It was like an anointing into the spirit of the civil rights movement. It was powerful. And it taught me even more about what the arts can do. I was always pushing it for the kids at school because one reason for all the absenteeism and the drop outs and disinterest in schooling was because there weren't many opportunities for creative expression in school. The arts offer this experience and so much more.

There is always something very special about your first play, your first love, your first anything. *Gospel at Colonus* was my first play. And *Legacy* in 2009 was to be my last, for reasons that I could never have predicted, and which will forever in my mind be a precursor to the awful events of 2010.

Life is a carousel of changes. You can fight these changes vehemently at every turn or humbly accept them as transitions in life. Either way, they are going to happen. I loved singing and I loved performing. I had also always been a physically fit, competitive person. For example, at the gym if the person next to me was bicycling for half an hour, I had to pedal for an hour. If the person next to me lifted ten-pound dumb bells, I had to double that weight with multiple repetitions. Why? Because as small children, my siblings and I were always told to be the best, to push ourselves to the limit. It took me awhile to figure out what my limits were and to let that be the barometer on how hard to push. One of my mantras had always been "the sky is the limit." But as we grow older and approach our twilight years, there is a physical limit to what our bodies can endure. I found that out soon enough.

The carousel of life was about to take me for a spin. Unbeknownst to me, I was on the verge of losing my precious voice—literally and figuratively—and even possibly my life. It began with a cruise to Puerto Rico, Antigua, St. Maarten and St. Thomas in the summer of 2009. Or rather, it began when the cruise ended.

I had gotten into the habit of treating myself to a Caribbean cruise as a reward for another year of hard work. As a principal of an inner city school, I expended an unbelievable amount of energy and personal sacrifice to meet the daily challenges. I favored a cruise line called Festival at Sea. This unique cruise with an African Twist catered primarily to African Americans with entertainment, activities and food from the Black culture.

In fact, when my own children were younger, our entire family went on a couple of three-day cruises down the California coast to Mexico. I remember on one particular trip Richard, my son, entertaining himself by creating a variety of "gotcha moments" with his video camera. He caught one of Monique dancing on deck. Maybe one day I will be able to watch that again.

Over the years, whether cruising with family or on my own I built relationships with other passengers, cruising regulars like myself. The fellowship with long-time friends and my newly developed onboard friendships were always like a breath of fresh air to me.

My cruise in the summer of 2009 was equally as enjoyable and rejuvenating as the ones in the past. It provided me with the mental, physical, and spiritual rest and relaxation that I had paid a pricey fee for. I ended the cruise refreshed and ready to face the new school year and the all-consuming responsibilities that awaited me.

Oddly, when my plane landed at the Sacramento International Airport, I noticed a hoarseness in my voice. As the week continued, the hoarseness turned my voice into a whisper. By the second week, I was on the phone with my physician. He chuckled. "Deborah, the cure for laryngitis is to refrain from talking." Easy for him to say. He wasn't principal of an elementary school where one's voice projected authority and commanded the control tower of daily operations.

I proceeded with my daily duties, apologizing to all I came in contact with for my vocal inadequacies. After another two weeks went by without any improvement, I suspected something else was happening, something not laryngitis. I had no idea what that "something" could possibly be, but I was feeling quite anxious to find out.

Once again I called my doctor. I told him that I wanted a chest x-ray and any other additional testing done that might be useful in determining what was going on with my voice. He acquiesced and ordered the requested testing. He also prescribed a drug for acid reflux disorder. I thought this was curious since I had never been tested for acid reflux, but I was so desperate for a healing that I would have taken anything at that point.

Two days later, I received a telephone call directly from the doctor. I knew this wasn't a good sign because usually I had to jump through hoops to talk to him. "Deborah, I'm going to refer you to a throat specialist for further testing on your vocal cords," he said.

"That serious?" I asked.

"Possibly. Yes. And, well, there's something else." I waited while he cleared his throat. "It's your chest x-ray."

"Is there a problem with my lungs?"

"Not your lungs. Your heart."

He went on to tell me that my heart was twice the size of a normal heart. I didn't seem to be processing what he was saying. I asked him what he meant, but he would only say that he didn't want to elaborate more on my condition until I was seen by a cardiologist. "We'll get you in immediately," he said. "What I can tell you is that very likely what you're experiencing is congestive heart failure."

Congestive Heart Failure? Not possible! I could outrun most people in my age group and many younger. I had exercised all of my life and watched the amount of fat that I consumed on a regular basis. My mind became a whirlwind of questions and second-guessing. I had never noticed any heart complications. Except for that one time I climbed the stairs in my son's house and I became so winded that I had to sit down for a few minutes. And yes, I had gotten dizzy and dropped to the floor a couple of months ago, but I had assumed that malfunction was due to the new contact lenses I had purchased the day before.

And well, thinking about it, there *was* the time I was walking through an Indian Casino and had to sit down to regroup a minute due to dizziness.

And that time on the cruise ship dance floor, when everyone was doing the quick-stepped Chicago Strut and some little voice in my head said don't do it, while an image of my heart came to mind. *Congestive heart failure?* That was for the elderly. *Congestive heart failure?* That was for fat people who didn't exercise or watch what they ate. Congestive heart failure was what my Aunt Marcella had died of. *Hell No!* And all I had wanted to know was why I had a prolonged case of laryngitis.

For the next two weeks my phone and answering machine were inundated with calls to set up appointments with specialists and for an array of testing like CT scans and MRI's. Trying to open a new school year and keep all of these appointments would present an insurmountable challenge even for a magician. I am a very private and proud person, which can be a good and bad thing. I wanted to keep my declining health a secret from the staff and my Parkway students. But signs of stress became quickly evident. My voice remained a whisper and with the new heart medication that was ordered for me, inevitable side effects took hold including fatigue.

It was at this point that I most valued the relationship with Angie, my office manager. I pulled her into my office and shared everything that I was going through. In addition, I explained that if any of my behaviors seemed weird to her, there was a substantial reason for it. We immediately made a plan that would allow me to take frequent breaks throughout the day and if anyone asked, trust me, this hot-blooded Latina had my back. Just like family.

While being bombarded with health issues like an atomic bomb, I made every effort to keep up with my daily routine and job obligations. So far, so good. No one seemed the wiser that my breathing was strained, my energy levels were depleting fast, and a clinical case of depression was beginning to set in.

October 9, 2009 was scheduled to be a big day for our school campus. The Board of Education had just hired a new superintendent, Sebastian Walton, and he was coming to visit Parkway School. This was my opportunity to showcase the learning environment, the students, and the staff that I was so proud of. Superintendent Walton wanted to make a cameo visit into several of the classrooms, and I made certain that the programs and the people that I felt were directly responsible for our ongoing successes were visited on his itinerary. My students were illuminating like the stars they were, and staff members were also excited about his visit.

His hour long stay required quite a bit of fast-paced walking that on any given day would typically have had little to no impact on me. I truly feel that to be an effective principal, one needs to be somewhat athletic to meet the daily demands and to monitor the daily instructional programs and operations. I was such a pro at this, even in my 50's, that when people referred to me in reports or in person, they would refer to me as that "energetic principal, or that "high-energy principal." I was so conditioned to move at a fast pace, that when I would vacation in the Bahamas the locals would whisper in my ear, "slow down," whenever I walked past.

Once I had completed the tour of our school with Superintendent Walton, and after he'd left the building, an episode began. I hurried to my office and fell onto a chair, hyperventilating. I began experiencing cold sweats and my skin felt clammy. "Girl, you don't look so good," Angie observed. For a woman as vain as I, this statement was not taken lightly. Once again, I told her to cover for me as I tried to relax and regroup in my office until this awkward feeling passed.

I stayed secluded behind closed doors for an hour. The symptoms did not subside. Now chest pains were included in the little fiasco and I honestly thought I was on the brink of having a heart attack. When Angie came to check on me, I tried to be as calm as possible so as not to frighten her. "Could you please call my son to take me to the emergency room? I've never felt quite like this before."

The ER staff took good care of me and determined that I was not having a heart attack but probably had had a negative reaction to all the new medications that I was taking. Unfortunately, during my first month of treatment, visits to the emergency room became quite frequent.

After all the heart testing was completed, I met with the throat surgeon for my vocal cord issues. He hypothesized that the most prominent reason for my vocal cord paralysis was due to thyroid cancer. "I think we should operate," he said. "We'll remove the left-side of your thyroid and three nodules that might also be culprits in paralyzing the vocal cord nerve." The surgery was scheduled for November 16th.

I informed staff and students at Parkway that surgery was needed to restore my voice. The District found an extremely competent retired administrator, Jocelyn Moore, to substitute for me. What lightened my load considerably was the genuine concern and support I received from my immediate family. Monique, Tamora, and Richard made sure everything on their calendars was set aside so they could be there for me. However, I felt it strange that, as the surgeons prepared to slice and dice me, all I could think about was how the school was doing.

When I woke up in the recovery room, I could only vaguely hear my doctor talking to me because I was so drowsy. However, I did hear the beautiful words, "no cancer," and I immediately sent a praise of thanks to the Lord. Family members came to visit me. At first, I couldn't read the odd looks on their faces—until I looked in the mirror. I was aghast to see that my throat had a huge, ugly, five-to-six-inch gash across it. I looked like I had been in a fight with the L.A. Slasher and I had lost.

Words cannot express how elated I felt after the surgery. It was the first time in three months that I heard my normal voice emanate from my mouth. My surgeon must be a miracle worker, I thought. All of my worst fears were put to rest. No cancer. And my signature voice was back. This was indeed a great day.

The next day, I was released from the hospital, and Monique brought me home to my loving family. My voice was still intact, and the pain from the incision was bearable due to my new little friend, Vicodin. Family and friends visited me that evening and I settled down in my bedroom, ready to embark on the road to recovery. That night, I prayed to God and thanked Him for a successful surgery.

The following morning Monique greeted me with her usual smile. "Good morning, Mama."

I open my mouth to return the greeting. Nothing came out. Not even a whisper escaped my lips. Panic set in as I realized my exaltations of success the previous day were premature.

I had always taken so much in life for granted. Walking, eating, working, and talking. Until I lost my ability to verbally communicate, I had no idea of how desperate the situation could be. Without a voice, I realized, I couldn't even call 911 to get help in the event of a heart attack. Months of laryngitis and now all of a sudden I had no voice at all. This was turning out to be a living, hellish nightmare.

I immediately emailed my doctor and he replied that he would check it out at my next appointment—in two weeks. *Two weeks?* What was I going to do for two weeks?

Monique at first thought my inability to talk was funny. "Did you hear that?" she would say. "Silence!" Or she would declare, "Peace at last!" But deep inside, I knew, she was concerned that this disability might be permanent or require additional surgery.

In order to communicate, I had to use a lot of body language, and I went through a multitude of post-its. Monique and Tamora, to thrust me into the 21st millennium, taught me how to text.

I quickly sank into a quagmire of depression. Crying uncontrollably, albeit silently, became a daily occurrence. My sisters, Ellouise and Beatrice, were constantly advising me to pray and trust in the Lord. All I could think of was *why me?* Wasn't I a good person? Didn't I try to speak up for what was right? Now I didn't have a political, physical, or any other kind of voice.

Monique became my guardian angel for those next two weeks. She took me to all of my doctors and business appointments and performed as my Voice. Other family members desperately tried to encourage me and even took me out in an effort to cheer me up. All of these activities were to no avail. You know how it is to go a movie and everyone is excitedly discussing the plot, events, and characters? Can you imagine what it would be like to have opinions, but when you try to express them no words come from your mouth? I was totally mute! So these outings had the opposite effect on me. I found my emotional state vacillating back and forth between a sense of hopelessness and anger as I continued to sink further and further into the abyss.

While experiencing the pain of recent surgery and the setback with my vocal cords, my weakened heart muscle was also in need of attention. I went to see my cardiologist, Dr. Harry Ingram, at Kaiser Permanente North, during this period of silence. Dr. Ingram could see the mental and physical anguish that I was in, and he increased my dosage of heart medication. My test results revealed that my heart was operating at only 20-25 percent of its capacity, and my ability to complete small tasks, such as walking from the parking lot to his office, became increasingly difficult.

In three short months, I had regressed from a vibrant, accomplished, school principal to a disabled, aging invalid with a double whammy—no voice and a failing heart. In my linear way of thinking, what made the situation even more horrendous to grasp was that none of my doctors could tell me *why* my body was failing me. It must be one of the seven plagues, I decided. Without hesitation, Dr. Ingram placed me on a medical leave of absence for a year.

Somehow, I had to find the words to inform the staff that indeed, I was ill and needed to pass the torch of leadership for the 2009-2010 school year. I prepared a memo and had it read at the next staff meeting. After expressing my heart-felt gratitude for the well wishes and the thoughtfulness that had been continually extended my way during my health challenges, I explained it this way:

"It amazes me how one day you can be on a Caribbean Cruise out-dancing and out-eating all of the passengers on board and then the next day a mysterious case of laryngitis appears. Then three weeks later, it is determined that it is not laryngitis at all, but possibly thyroid cancer. Then, two weeks later you have surgery and thank God it is not thyroid cancer but a left-sided vocal cord paralysis that will require additional surgery in three months. During this problem-solving process with the vocal cords, the physicians discover that you have a life-altering disease called cardiomyopathy, which is an enlarged heart that is working at 20-25% of the capacity of a normal heart! I share all this personal and private information to reveal the difference a day can make."

I told them that through it all, I was "optimistic, getting stronger each day, and missing my Parkway Family immensely." I thank the Parkway Dream Team and "especially my babies for continuing with our tradition of academic and social excellence in my absence."

Then I said:

The Last Portrait: A Psalm For Monique

"All of my life, I have felt that I had to be a 'Super Woman' and when I am given an assignment, *I try to give it my all* - emotionally, spiritually, and physically. To my chagrin, the physical component has taken its toll. My doctors have placed me on medical leave for twelve months to re-adjust my life-style, try a series of new medications to treat my existing illnesses, and to allow me additional time to heal from a second surgery. Knowing my God and me, we can accomplish this feat in about six months. Oops, that is that Super Woman talking again. (*Smile!*) Please continue to support, encourage, and love each other as a family with a relentless focus on stopping the educational failure for children of color and children of poverty."

I reminded them that my favorite song was "Everything Must Change" (by George Benson); and that although, I was unable to be with them physically during the upcoming school year, I wanted them to know that my spirit and "BIG heart" beat in every inch of the school and "most affectionately for my babies."

Lastly, I quoted a stanza from a favorite poem, *Still I Rise*, by Maya Angelou:

"Just like moons and like suns,
With the certainty of tides,
Just like hopes springing high,
Still I'll rise!"

When the 2010 school year commenced, my continuing health challenges finally forced me to retire from my job as principal of Parkway Elementary. On November 1, 2010 I was granted disability retirement from the school district due to my heart condition. No more running from classroom to classroom, supervising the school grounds, and playing basketball in heels for me. My professional career as an elementary school principal was over. Trying to maintain a positive attitude, I focused more on my glass being half-full instead of half-empty. It was time to think about how I was going reinvent myself for the second half of my life.

With my professional experiences and life lessons, I honestly believed that I still had a lot to offer in serving our community. Volunteering at Kaiser hospital and returning to school as a life-long learner were my baby steps in reinventing myself.

During my illness, Monique and I experienced a total role reversal. She became the mother and I the child. She had gone to Western Career College (now Carrington College) and was a licensed medical assistant. Her business cards, printed on a powder blue card infused with white clouds, were labeled: "*Walking By Faith, Monique Nelson, Caregiver.*" Her spiritual gift was to uplift those in need. When her Uncle Rick, my sister Beatrice's husband, was dying from cancer it was Monique who cared for him and gave her aunt a much-needed break. On another occasion, my sister's neighbor was dying of cancer and it was Monique who quieted him and witnessed his last breath. And true to her talents, she brought an impressive amount of professionalism and love to *my* bedside.

Whenever I would delve into an abyss of self-pity and negativity, she would cuss me out and encourage me to keep moving forward. The truth is that my daughter saved my life. I had given up the will to live and she would not allow it. She became not exclusively my daughter but a good friend. Daily, I would make depressing comments about how I wanted her to be happy in case of my imminent death. Repeatedly she would say, "Mama, you aren't going anywhere. I won't allow it!"

One Sunday during that period I cornered Monique and shared with her what I wanted her to do upon my passing. Suddenly Monique grew ashen. She backed up against my bedroom wall.

"Mama," she said, "Sometimes the child goes before the parent."

I shivered but said nothing. Somehow the Spirit just knows what is forthcoming.

CHAPTER 8

Are You There?

I GRIEVED THE LOSS OF my voice. A unique voice, my children told me, that no one else in the universe could duplicate. The voice that had a quirky little laugh at the dumbest of jokes. The voice that disciplined my own three children and hundreds of other children in the public school system. The voice that also expressed a deep-rooted passion and love for my offspring and the offspring of others. The voice that would solemnly pray, with the faith that those prayers would be answered. The voice that challenged authority and the injustices that I saw taking place in the political arena. The voice that talked to family, friends and neighbors on a wide variety of topics. An indistinguishable voice, I was told, that could be identified in a crowd or without even seeing my face. A voice that mirrored the voice of my mother in song. I missed—still miss—singing with groups and performing in community plays and musicals. Because, now, I had no voice!

As a preacher's daughter, I was always taught to trust and love the Lord. A good Christian never questions God but obediently accepts His will. At this fissure in my life, I just was not feeling it. I felt abandoned. I felt betrayed. What had I done that was so displeasing to His sight? Face it; I am not like the Biblical Job, someone who falls silent before God, gifted with an unfailing faith. But when I believed I was at rock bottom, when I could not see my way out of a situation, when I was in need of a break-through, the long and short of it was, all I really had was God.

To keep from losing my mind, I began to write poetry again.

ARE YOU THERE?
(By Deborah Nelson)

Life is full of ups and downs
Decisions to be made, yet no peace to be found.
Are You There?

Family torn apart, finances are bleak.
Hope is dim and moral values are weak.
Are You There?

Standing on the promises of Jesus
But questioning is He truly there for us.
Are You There?

Diseases abound, political corruption everywhere,
Children are hungry and lost, justice just isn't fair.
Are You There?

Even those who have been faithful to You
Are confused and wondering what to do.
Are You There?

Mama dies of cancer, Daddy dies of cancer; can't find a cure.
Trust in Me and you will be free, oh sure.
Are You There?

The wicked seem to prosper,
The faithful seem to falter.
Are You There?

The doctor's prognosis is grim,
Scared, fearful and looking mighty slim.
Are You There?

The Last Portrait: A Psalm For Monique

What doesn't kill you makes you stronger.
How strong do you have to be? Just can't go on any further.
Are You There?

My direct connection is supposed to be prayer.
But the line is broken. Can't get a response, I swear.
Are You There?

Tried to make a difference but it wasn't to your liking.
Work without faith, I must still be lacking.
Are You There?

Don't know which way to turn or what to do.
See no way out; constantly blue.
Are You There?

Everything I've worked for gone up in smoke.
Living in these earthly conditions just is no joke.
Are You There?

Mama said "Lean On His Everlasting Arms".
But the confusion in my head sets off alarms.
Are You There?

Daddy said, "You are the Truth and the Light.
Please don't give up on the good fight."
Are You There?

Another test, another trial to test my waning faith.
The devil rejoices and makes me saith,
Are You There?

I need salvation, I need peace of mind.
I need to see a miracle, You, I want to find.
Are You There?

Fearful of living, Fearful of dying
No words are inspiring. No Angels are flying.
Are You There?

You said You'd never leave me.
You said my soul would be free.
Are You There?

I can't see you, I can't touch you.
I'm falling in an abyss of doubt.
Are You There?

Don't let the devil win. Be my eternal friend.
Lead Me, Guide Me to the end.
Are You There?

Something has touched my heart.
Something has touched my soul.
Are You There?

Something has guided me to the Word. It said,
"Take heart, I have overcome the world."
Was It You? Are You There?

This Voice says, "Restore your faith, renew your faith, believe and trust.
If you want me there, this is a must!"

I never left you. You left me. I can't wait to accept you into our holy family tree.

The Last Portrait: A Psalm For Monique

You ask, "Are You There?' You can't be talking to me.
Because by your Faith you are saved and there is no other way to be.

Yes, I am here. To hold your hand and guide you through.
But trials and tribulations are the test one must go thru.
To build character, to be a witness to God's mercy and grace.
Because He offers you Everlasting Life in a magnificent holy place.

Are You There? Yes, since the beginning of time.
But you cannot tap into my greatness until you're a true friend of mine.

I hear your cries. I feel your pain. But that's your test not mine to endure.
To prepare you for the Kingdom of Heaven with a spirit that is pure.

No pain, No gain, what can I say?
My Son had to do it, He paved the way.
I will not save you from all of life's aches and pains.
But I promise to be with you, and with Faith you will never be the same.

Yes, I'm Here.

See the wind gently blowing through the trees.
See the stars shining brightly on thee.
See the flowers bloom and the waves touching the shores.
Know the Blood of Jesus was shed so you don't have to fear death anymore.

Yes, I'm Here.

I'm omnipotent, omnipresent, and omniscient.
And through it all I offer love and salvation to the saint.

Yes, I'm Here

I'm the Guiding Light, The Rock, King of Kings, Lord of Lords and the Messiah,
Yahweh, Jehovah, Elahim, El-Shaddai, An-Rahman and Allah.
Regardless of what you call me
Regardless of the peace you seek
Without relentlessly trusting and believing,
Your life isn't really worth living.

Yes, I'm Here, I'm There, I'm Everywhere.

The storms will come and the storms will go.
But my Love and Word is forever more.
So, yes, I'm Here, I'm There, I'm Everywhere.
But My Child, Are You Really There?

Will you let go of your worldly ways?
Crucify self and sacrifice many days
To do the Kingdom work and spread the good news.
That a new day is dawning and it will start with you.

With Me Here and You Here I can certainly guarantee
That one day you will see Christ and joyously worship Me.
   "Let Everything That Has Breath, Praise the Lord."
    ~Psalm 150:6

There had been talk of doing surgery to repair my damaged vocal cords—a step I was working hard to avoid. With the help of a speech therapist, I began making incremental progress on regaining my voice.

 From the moment I entered her office in October, Ms. B. had exuded with positivity. When I despaired because the doctors warned that I may never speak again, Ms. B. would declare, "Yes, you will." When I was depressed because the volume of my voice seemed not to improve, she would say. "Yes, it has."

When I told her that one of my most earnest prayers was *not* to have vocal cord implant surgery, she gave me exercises designed to strengthen the vocal cords. Ms. B. even encouraged me to sing a little each day. This was probably the most difficult exercise because prior to all this I had sung like a melodious nightingale. Now I sounded like a raspy nightmarish gale. But we were in the vocal cord box marathon, and Ms. B. was doing everything possible to help me improve.

The only component she could not fix was *time*. If my vocal nerve was to regenerate and heal itself, it could take up to one year. The vocal cord repair and implant surgery had been scheduled for three months after my thyroid surgery. Ms. B, being fully aware of my desire to avoid surgery, encouraged me to ask for more time. I told my doctor that I would like to monitor my progress for six months instead of three. He graciously agreed. But realistically, to wait for an entire year without an efficient voice was proving longer than I could bear.

While I was on medical leave, a great distraction for me was to stay busy. I still monitored the educational program at Parkway from afar. I worked to coordinate various enrichment programs such as Literacy Days, an arts education program, a Black Studies program, and our annual Multicultural Extravaganza. These duties were a welcome relief from thinking about all my health issues, which seem to continually take a downward spiral. The staff and administrators at Parkway kept me apprised of the school's progress and encouraged me to continue with my leadership responsibilities even if I physically could not be there.

The lack of normalcy in my new lifestyle made the void in my heart even greater for my extended Parkway family. I missed the challenges of daily operations but I especially missed the children. On one of my return visits to meet with the site administrators, the word spread quickly that I was on campus. The children flooded the office and provided me with the familiar hugs that I had grown accustomed to and now needed more than ever.

It occurred to me that the old adage, "What doesn't kill you makes you stronger," was one I needed to grasp for dear life. And I didn't know whether to be comforted or dismayed by the famous Bernard Ighner lyric, "Everything Must Change. Nothing Stays the Same."

Having a severe case of dilated cardiomyopathy along with the left side of my vocal box being paralyzed required a plethora of lifestyle changes and modifications. The regime of drug therapy included beta blockers, diuretics, ace inhibitors, levothyroxine, simvastatin, 81mg of baby aspirin—and a friendly dose of lorazepam to help decrease the panic attacks that I frequently experienced. There were so many pills and the doses would increase as my tolerance level permitted. My best friend was the pillbox organizer; otherwise an overdose or under-dose could easily take place.

I did my homework on the pros and cons of all these drugs. Some of the possible side effects could include a high potassium levels, swelling of the face, tongue, and lips, dizziness, a slow heart rate, and the list goes on and on and on. An ironic aspect of the drug world is that for every side effect one medicine can potentially produce, the doctors can always prescribe another drug to counter that side effect—what I call the "ping pong effect" of pill-taking.

Dr. Ingram assigned a "Chronic Condition Manager" to help me through the maze of life-style adjustments. Jorge Garcia had years of experience working with patients who suffered from congestive heart failure. He would call me on a weekly basis to check on my blood pressure, weight, diet and medications.

Whenever I'd complain about changes to my lifestyle or my medication regime, Jorge replied with compassion, "I want to do whatever it takes to keep you living longer." I couldn't argue with that logic.

With all the bad news I was receiving regarding my heart and my health, the question for me became: at what point do I call 911 for a cardiac arrest? What are the symptoms? I knew it differed for men and women and even from person to person. It seemed that every little ache, pain or change in my body elevated my awareness and had me questioning, *is this the day?*

Jorge had an offbeat sense of humor and could be painstakingly honest when asked a potentially explosive question. As I was trying to reorganize my life to deal with this "heart thing," I contacted and joined Medic Alert. This nonprofit organization helps to relay your personal health record to first responders in the event that you are unresponsive during a medical emergency. In addition, I was informed that through my house alarm service I could purchase a device which could be activated in case I was at home alone and had a heart attack.

So I asked Jorge what he thought about me purchasing an emergency alarm device. He replied with a straight face, "Deborah, with your heart condition, by the time you hit the floor you will be dead."

That may have sounded a little frightening, but from a medical viewpoint he was absolutely right. My diseased heart muscle made me a prime candidate for the "Sudden Death Syndrome," which happens when the electrical instability of the heart is compromised.

Nevertheless, I told Monique about Jorge's comment and we fell onto the floor laughing hysterically. One has to have a sense of humor during a crisis. And this situation I found myself in was the most bizarre of crises.

Another modification that needed to take place was to my exercise program and the amount of activity I was allowed on a day-to-day basis. In the past, I would work out daily, or at least four times a week, at 24-Hour Fitness, a local gym. My exercise program would include an hour of cardio and an hour of resistance or weight lifting for the upper and lower body. Unless I was in a full lather at the end of a session, I had always considered myself a failure with that day's routine.

As my Chronic Condition Manager, it was Jorge's job to help me modify my routine. I was to start with a two-minute cardio program that gradually increased to a "comfortable" level for my heart. It was five months since my diagnosis and to my chagrin all I could do was thirty minutes of cardio on a stationary bike with no tension on it whatsoever. I found myself embarrassed when I'd run into associates I had known for years at the gym; it bothered me they might witness this pitiful workout routine and hear my wimpy little voice. Was it just my imagination or were they looking at me in wonderment as if I had lost my mind? I could see in their eyes that they were dying to ask me what was wrong, but they were too polite or uncomfortable to approach me. To cap it all, they would see me parking in the handicapped parking space with my newly acquired handicapped sticker.

A less pleasant modification that I had to make was related to the pooper-scooper. At the time I lived with a hundred-and-twelve-pound, tan and black Anatolian Shepard named Cheyenne. I'd had him for five years, and trust me he was in great need of a Dog Whisperer. He was your typical alpha male and challenged me on every command that I tried to make. Because of the cardio-myopathy, my relationship even with the dog had to change. His roughhousing and play fighting with me had to stop.

Part of my daily regimen was to get the shovel and collect his poop from the yard. This mammoth dog not only ate like a horse but excreted like a horse as well. When I attempted to complete this daily chore, I'd start to hyperventilate and experience chest pains and a scary shortness of breath. At times, I couldn't complete the task and wondered if I needed to call 911. After a few attempts of trial and error, I modified this obligation by purchasing a child's plastic shovel and bending at the knees instead of stooping over when cleaning up after this woman's best friend. Eventually, I found a good home for Cheyenne with people who had the ability and the energy to take care of him in a way I no longer could.

One of the most difficult adjustments for me was the necessity to change my eating habits, particularly when it came to salt. Sodium, of course, can cause the body to retain excess water, which puts extra strain on the heart and increases blood pressure. Jorge was so committed to improving the lives of heart patients that even his voicemail message would candidly state, "Remember, salt is your enemy!"

He recommended I take a class for congestive heart failure patients in which we had to do a simulation of shopping for low-sodium products at the grocery store. Be assured, this was no easy feat for me. However, the shopping exercise did increase my awareness of the ridiculously high amount of salt the average American consumes each day. What an eye opener this experience was for me, especially since it was a long-time family tradition to eat southern-fried, crispy chicken several times a week. I just loved that stuff! I could eat a whole yard bird by myself. But this tasty habit had to change if my heart failure situation was to improve. Some sacrifices were quite painful but not as painful as the obvious alternative.

Monique took up the challenge with me, and we learned to read the labels at the grocery store. Gleefully, we cheered whenever we'd find food items that were not frozen, canned, or preserved in salt and possessed zero sodium content. I began shopping more at Trader Joe's and Whole Foods and going out to restaurants less and less.

The last life-style modification was to keep my cell phone on my person at all times.

CHAPTER 9

That Rogue Heart of Mine

GRADUALLY, MY WHISPERY VOICE CAME back. However, the nerve that operates the left side of my vocal box remained paralyzed. In a small room you could understand what I was saying; but in a crowded room, such as a restaurant, I would have to constantly repeat myself and add some body language to get my point across. Still, I was extremely grateful to have this piece of a voice as opposed to having the no-voice situation that I experienced the previous week. The plan was to wait for six months to see if the nerve near my voice box would regenerate itself. If the nerve remained paralyzed, another surgery would be performed to insert a voice implant.

I took my heart medication as instructed and adhered to the low-sodium diet. Still unable to walk and work as I had in the past, nevertheless I convinced myself that I was improving. My next appointment with Dr. Ingram deflated that belief. He told me that my ejection fraction rate (a measure of how well the heart is pumping out blood) was still too dangerously low to effectively pump blood throughout my body, even with the medication. He was considering implanting a biventricular pacemaker and defibrillator into my chest to assist my heart. The pacemaker would regulate my heartbeat and the defibrillator would shock me back to life in the event of cardiac arrest.

This was an idea that would take some getting used to. With the potential of a vocal implant and a cardio implant, I was on my way to becoming the new "Bionic Woman" who could never go through airport security again without causing a fuss. All *I* wanted to do was to be left alone. I call this period of my life "the period of I want." I wanted my voice back. I wanted my heart back to its normal size. I wanted my health back. I wanted my job back. I wanted my life back!

Although I had been divorced for twenty-three years at that point, I have to admit that when I was down and out my former husband, Richard, was always there for me. During those trying health times he would wait long hours at the hospital, take me on mini-vacations to the Bay Area and Vegas, and (too often) take me on field trips to our favorite local hangouts—the Indian Casinos. The thing about casinos is, it doesn't matter if you are on crutches, in a wheel chair, or have an oxygen tank you are still welcome to hang out and gamble. My Ex constantly went out of his way to entertain me and to show his genuine concern for my well-being. He would endure my poor sportsmanship behavior when I lost to him in Gin Rummy, and he even talked about some of his annoying behaviors that extended back forty years ago. We made a lousy couple but we have been, all along, best friends.

My children had always regarded me as the driven, strong, uncompromising "Super Woman" who sees all, handles all, and most importantly never was sick. This crisis of failing health and the reality that even mom is a mere mortal was an eye opener for them, but also brought out the best in them.

Richard, my eldest, was—and still is—an adventurous, optimistic young man. At the time, he was running his father's bookstore at the Sacramento International Airport. He's also the proud father of my picture-perfect, then-three-year-old grandson, Rayonne. The apple of grandma's eye, Rayonne was and is a triple threat: handsome, intelligent and very athletic. Richard takes great pride in masking his emotions; however, during that period of my illness, I started to see a change taking place within him. He was stepping up to the plate and willingly accepted his leadership role in the family. We were probably a doctor's worst nightmare because we would do our research and type lists of questions to be answered related to my health issues. We were so thorough in our investigations that at times the doctors would have to research our questions themselves before supplying answers. I learned so much from my son during this process. And even with his busy schedule, I could count on Richard to visit frequently and to show me no mercy when he challenged me in a game of cards or dominoes.

For Christmas that year—2009—Richard surprised me with a gift certificate to the Esthetics Salon. I was so preoccupied with all my health issues it wasn't until late in February that I got around to making an appointment to cash in on his gift.

As I was reading the gift card that identified what type of beauty treatment had been purchased, I couldn't believe my eyes! Here I was, suffering from congestive heart failure, taking a regimen of medications and adhering to a low-sodium diet and what had my son gifted me with? The certificate was not for your typical massage—but for a SALT SCRUB! *Oh. My. God.* Was my son trying to kill me? With salt? He knew that my biggest enemy was that little white crystal. I immediately envisioned myself going into cardiac arrest on the spa table surrounded by a kiddy-aged masseuse who had no idea what to do about it.

I called the salon and explained that I was a heart patient and that the salt scrub might present some health issues for me. The young lady on the end of the phone recommended that I try the sugar scrub instead.

Thoroughly relieved, I agreed to the change. The last comment made by the receptionist was, "Rest assured, I will make certain that your therapist is aware of your condition and there will absolutely be no salt!"

I gratefully thanked her and eagerly waited until that Tuesday afternoon to receive this immensely needed spa treatment.

Tuesday arrived cold, wet, and rainy. My mood matched the oppressive feeling of the day. I dressed comfortably and thought ahead with some anticipation to the sugar scrub I was about to experience. During my lifetime, I had had numerous massages—Swedish, Thai, and even sensual *(don't tell my kids!)*. But never a sugar scrub. I had especially relished the Thai massage I'd had with Tamora in Southern California. For only forty dollars this three-foot-tall woman massaged us from head to toe using her hands, elbows, knees and feet, and twisted and turned our bodies like some sort of contortionist. By the time we were done being Kung Fu-ed by this no nonsense woman, we felt amazingly balanced and quite relaxed.

Once at the Esthetics Salon, I was introduced to my therapist, a petite Latina named Erma. I was instructed to change into a spa robe and slippers. Then I was taken to a tranquil, mood-setting waiting room. Erma brought a huge bowl of hot, sudsy water to soak my feet in while I drank lemon water and listened to New Age music. After a while, she took me to my personal wet room which was dimly lit and exuded with the ambience of relaxation. Soft music reminiscent of waterfalls set the mood, accented with a faint aroma of vanilla candles. Erma once again asked me to change, this time handing me a very tiny, disposable, paper-like thong.

"What the heck is this for?" I asked.

Erma patiently replied, "It is to cover your lower body so we can proceed with the beauty treatment."

"Is this *all* I'll be wearing?" I exclaimed, blushing with embarrassment.

She nodded politely. I thought to myself, "I am almost sixty years old. I do not wear thongs. My hotty-totty daughters wear thongs! But I don't. Not me."

But Erma only stood there waiting. So, I obediently adhered to her request, slipped on the paper thong, and laid face down on the table. I wondered, "What's going to happen next?"

Erma left the room for a moment and came back carrying all the materials, minerals, and aromatic oils that she would be using, including a large bowl of something white and crystalline.

"What is that?" I asked.

"It is salt," she said.

"Oh. No. Nope. No salt," I insisted. I quickly explained that I was a congestive heart failure patient and that I had told the receptionist of my condition when I made my appointment. Erma apologized, saying she had not been informed about any special instructions related to my appointment and said that of course we would do the sugar scrub.

She left briefly to discuss the situation with her boss then returned with a bowl of white granular-looking yet coarse-in-texture sugar. As I lay there on the table in this *Me Jane, You Tarzan* thong, I became very aware of my nakedness. I felt somewhat self-conscious of the cellulite on my thighs and this aging body that was sprawled out on the table like a nude mannequin.

Normally, I am way too modest to be exposed in this manner. However, once my therapist started to apply the sugar scrub between my toes and on every part of my body up to my hair on my head, all of my insecurities and inhibitions quickly vanished.

From what I had read on salt and sugar scrubs, I knew that the primary purpose was to exfoliate the skin. In addition, it hydrates the skin because of the combination of ingredients used and leaves the skin feeling soft and fragrant. What I didn't know was how damn good it would feel! When she finished the backside of my body, Erma told me to turn over and she continued to work, this time on my front.

Erma had no intimation that this beauty treatment was actually quite spiritual for me. It was a perfect setting for meditating. I can remember every sound and smell that made this sugar scrub some kind of wonderful. I even had time to talk to God while on the table. The sugar scrub therapy felt like a healing for my aching soul and my discouraged spirit as much as for my body. I have never, before or since, experienced anything so stimulating, so totally rejuvenating. It was a renewal of the spirit. This was just what the doctor ordered!

Usually in my life, to escape from the numerous trials that I have faced, I take pride in my ability to have an out-of-body experience. Being out of body for me is a form of escapism from a traumatic experience or thought. The best way to explain it is that my body goes on autopilot because I can no longer control the pain or discomfort. It is a self-defense mechanism of numbness when I cannot take anymore. Since childhood it has been one of my strategies to deal with difficult situations. It feels like a floating sensation where I am no longer in my physical body but in the spiritual realm of peace. I find it especially helpful when mental anguish is abundant. When I had all those multiple surgeries and heath challenges, I called upon it. Facing the challenges of being a single parent, I called upon it. During the painful years of Monique's murder trial, I would frequently call upon it. And especially, while trying to daily cope with her death and the loneliness in my life, I call upon it still. Some may call it daydreaming, fantasizing, or whatever—but it works for me.

I can also undergo an out-of-body experience to express when I am euphoric. The most notable occurrence was when I witnessed the joy on

Monique's face the moment she saw Jayden for the first time. *Wow!* The only thing I can say is that my out-of-body experiences are not of this world but rather are spiritual in nature. It is grace and mercy.

However, on this day—at the Esthetics spa—I wanted to remain within my broken body to fully enjoy the complete essence of this divine sense of calm. As Erma expertly worked my body she was more than a spa therapist; she had become my psychotherapist—a psychotherapist with magical fingers that not only massaged my physical body but totally relaxed my overworked neural and emotional system.

And then, just when I knew this special feeling couldn't get any better, Erma proceeded to give me a much-needed massage with the most fantastic lavender-smelling oil. I had died and gone to Heaven.

Surely this massage must be the end of the treatment? I had been there for at least an hour and a half. I was so relaxed that I didn't give a hoot about work, my illness, or anything troubling me. *Oh my God!* It wasn't over yet! Erma took me to the steam room as the culminating event in this marathon of pleasure.

Richard was a Godsend for having the foresight and thoughtfulness to provide me with such a treat. I think of Erma not as a great therapist but the Goddess of Komboloi. *Komboloi* is a Greek term used to describe a means for meditation, calming pain, and pleasure for our senses. This special and unique experience at the spa was desperately needed as the first of March quickly approached when I had a scheduled appointment with Dr.Ingram to determine if my heart capacity had improved.

Tamora was residing in Los Angeles County at the time. She had a certain amount of flexibility in her schedule, and, per her own admission, "loves her Mama." So she enthusiastically made plans to be in Sacramento with me as much as possible. She accumulated exponential points on her frequent flyer miles coming and going to accommodate my surgeries and monitor my progress.

During my road to recovery, I even visited her in Los Angeles where she took me to the zoo and to the breathtaking beach. The walk was way too strenuous for me in my delicate condition, but she was prepared for my limitations. She had borrowed a wheelchair from a friend to allow me the opportunity to fully enjoy my day. She said, "Mama, you pushed me in a stroller for a year and now I get to return the favor." Although she was thrilled to help out her ailing mother, inwardly I felt overwhelmingly inadequate in my inability to be the strong, mother figure in her eyes.

Tamora shares my passion for writing poetry and for expressing herself through the written word. While I was convalescing, I would find notes throughout the house which she had addressed to me. I found this one on the refrigerator:

Too Blessed To Be Stressed
Remember, we didn't come this far to stop now☺
Things to do:

1. Take a class.
2. Start Your Own Business. (Deborah's Consulting!)
3. A little cardio every day.
4. Travel.

Remember:

A. Your Family Loves You.
B. You're going to grow old with your grandchildren.
C. You are AMAZING!
D. SMILE! It can heal everything. ☺

      I Love You,
      Tamora

I found this one on the kitchen countertop:

When You Wake Up
When you wake up in the morning and take a look at yourself, don't look at the scar that you have from surgery.

Think about the impact that you've had on other people's lives
and the scars that you've healed.
Try not to get wrapped up in a profession that you've had.
Think about all the things yet to come.
In my eyes, you've always been Superwoman.
You've always seen past your obstacles and have overcome your challenges.
So, Mama, you can't stop now!
Everything in life is a process that we have to take step-by step.
In my eyes, you're Superwoman.
I could of never done all the things that you've accomplished.
You're Superwoman not because of your career, but because of who <u>you are.</u>
The most beautiful, intelligent, and strong woman that I've ever known.
This is just stage one, and we will get through it together.
You don't have cancer. You have your family and we will be here with you always.
So, mama, let's get through stage one.
Superwoman, it's time to wake up!
I love you with all my heart and soul.
Tamora ☺

How did this young woman get so wise beyond her years? Tamora and Richard were both incredibly generous and invaluable in their support during my health crisis. But it was Monique, the youngest of the three, who had the training and experience in the health field to be my day-to-day caregiver. Although she had a year-old toddler in tow, she took remarkable care of her mother.

Her knowledge base—just knowing what questions to ask—and her persistence in getting answers from my physicians were instrumental to my healing process. She was knowledgeable about how and when to take my blood pressure, the pros and cons of various medications, and the many symptoms of illnesses related to my case. She also possessed an intuitive sixth sense about when I was feeling down or just not quite my usual upbeat self. I did not have to tell her. She could read my face like a book. When she had the slightest inkling that something was not quite right with me emotionally, she would bring over little busy-bee Jayden for a visit with Grandma. That was just the medicine needed to brighten my day.

On February 26th of 2010 I went to see my speech therapist again. And once again, Ms. B. played the role as my enthusiastic personal cheerleader. To me it seemed that my voice had not improved at all. The same embarrassment in public places and on the telephone with that breathy raspy voice continued. However, Ms. B. could always find a light in the tunnel.

When I greeted her with a whispery, "Good Morning," she excitedly replied, "Oh, I hear more voice!" I looked at her like she was crazy.

Then she proceeded to try and take pictures of my vocal cords and record the sounds of sporadic EEEEEEE's. She stuck an endoscope—a thin flexible tube with a tiny camera attached to the end—down my throat, which causes a gagging sensation for the unfortunate patient. As she scanned the images, she clinically reported that she saw movement from my left vocal cord. Not great but movement. Enough so that she gladly reported she would upgrade my vocal status from "paralysis" to "paresis."

Paralysis means the complete loss of nerve input to a muscle resulting in complete loss of vocal cord function. Paresis means partial paralysis of the nerve input to the vocal cord. Paresis suggests that hope for a natural recovery is good. This diagnosis justified waiting from four to ten months to see if the vocal fold paresis/paralysis resolved itself and whether my voice would improve on its own. I had noticed that I could now sing better than I could talk. The upgrade of my vocal progress to paresis was fantastic news because it meant the possibility of one less surgery.

Proud of the manner in which I was following all of Dr. Ingram's and Jorge's instructions, I became fanatical about adhering to the low-sodium diet. I faithfully took my vast number of pills, walked daily, exercised at the gym at a moderate pace at least three times a week, and strived to live a stress-free life—as stress-free as a chronically ill person can be. I monitored my blood pressure and weight daily. The result of this structured and well-disciplined life style was that I felt better! I had more energy and was ready to return to work.

Ever the good son, Richard escorted me to my next appointment with Dr. Ingram. I always believe in dressing the part for any event, and this was an important event. So I wore a lilac satin shirt with purple leggings and my black and purple coat to the appointment. I was looking good and feeling good!

The first step was to have an echocardiogram done to complete the study of my heart. The technician was cordial, professional, and very thorough in her duties. While she studied and monitored the pacing of my heart, I watched her every facial expression intently. Although, I do not have the expertise to interpret the various sounds and images that were being projected on the screen, I could try to read the technician's body language for clues to the results. This woman was very controlled and did not reveal any facial expressions or emotions for me to read. However, in the middle of the examination, she exhaled a very slow, exhaustive, and what I interpreted as a disappointed sigh. I ignored it, completed my echocardiogram, and proceeded to go next door to Dr. Ingram's office to discuss the results.

When Dr. Ingram entered the room we exchanged civil niceties and talked about everything but my heart. About ten minutes later, he reminded me that the main purpose for my visit this day was to figure out if my diseased heart was responding to the medication. I nodded. I was sure it had.

"Deborah, according to today's echocardiogram, your heart has grown two additional centimeters," he said. "Your heart muscle is now at eight centimeters."

I was shocked. That was way too large!

In addition, he told me, the lower right and left chambers were not synchronized, which was the culprit in the poor lower ejection fraction rate—the squeezing of the heart to move the blood throughout the body.

"How could this be?" Richard asked. "She's followed every bit of advice and taken all of her medications without fail."

"The medications don't seem to be making a difference. I think we need a more aggressive approach," Dr. Ingram advised. He stated that the next step would be the biventricular device implant he had mentioned before. It was no longer a matter of choice for me if I wanted to live. The reality was my life was now in greater danger than it had been prior to treatment. The implantation was a must!

At this point, fear started to overwhelm every atom in my body. The reality that I could die from this heart condition was paralyzing. Dr. Ingram said he would contact another specialist at Mercy Hospital who would take responsibility for implanting the biventricular device into my chest. Numerous thoughts raced through my mind and I could no longer hold back the tears. Dr. Ingram assured me that this device could help with the squeezing action of the heart and shock me back from the inevitable cardiac arrest. However, he warned, it could not shrink this stubborn rogue heart of mine.

In an effort to insulate myself from these new realities, I had Richard drop me off for a pedicure and a manicure. All I wanted was a little escapism, to relax and not think about the challenges in front of me. Nice try, but to no avail. The results of the tests and the limited future treatment options kept going in and out of my mind. It took every ounce of my being to hold it together in this public place and stay in control of my flood of emotions.

Once I got home, the meltdown started. I screamed and cried until I became an empty vessel. When I would try to regroup, the uncontrollable sobbing and grieving started all over again. Richard called each of my family members to update them on my lack of progress and to warn them not to come by the house just yet.

Monique, however, chose not to heed to his advice. She used her key and let herself in. As soon as I saw her, I accused her of invading my privacy—this was my personal meltdown. I ordered her to leave because I did not want to be bothered by anyone. I just couldn't act brave any longer. Without a word she obeyed my command and left; and I continued with my wailing and feelings of despair and self-pity.

The Last Portrait: A Psalm For Monique

My sister Beatrice repeatedly called and left messages on my cell phone, which I refused to answer. Tamora called from Southern California. I did answer her call, but only to tell her that I would call her back. I just wanted to be left alone!

About an hour later, I heard a lawn mower in the front yard. I suspected it was Richard and went to wash my face and drop some Visine into my teary, red eyes. Then I heard a strange knock at the front door. Puzzled, I opened the door and there, to my surprise, stood my precious grandson, Rayonne. Richard always knew how to get me out of a *funk*. Use my grandchild. Rayonne showed me two of his new toys and pointed to show me that his father was cutting the lawn. Not wanting my grandson to see me in such a depressed state, I forced myself to liven up and entertain him on his visit. After an hour or so, I couldn't fake it anymore; I went to lie down on my bed and Richard and Rayonne left.

Later, I texted Monique to apologize for kicking her out of the house. "It's okay, Mama," she said. "Just let me know when I can come over."

Tamora couldn't wait any longer. She called me again. I succumbed to yet another total meltdown on the phone with her and was completely inaudible. I tried to talk through the tears, but nothing but gibberish came out of my mouth. Tamora calmly and pointedly told me that she was going to give me two days to respond to this sense of loss in any manner that I deemed necessary, crying, screaming, anger, solitude, or whatever.

"Two days, Mama. Then you have to get on with the business of living—by whatever means necessary."

The following day, the surgeon's office called to set the appointment for the surgery. They wanted to do it immediately; but after a short pause, I stated boldly that I needed to take a trip to Las Vegas that weekend. And I needed to make arrangements for my daughter to be my caregiver again.

"This device is something that has the ability to save your life," the shocked scheduler reminded me.

"This may be true," I replied. "But this decision is a major adjustment in my life and I need a little more time to relax and reflect on this serious move. What if I die on the operating table? I've given quite a bit of thought to the difference between living a quality life and just living a long life. And while I want to live, I won't give up the quality. Please allow me a couple more days to get my mindset prepared for this procedure."

He agreed to postpone the surgery until the middle of the month. On March 5th, I met the specialist from Mercy Hospital who would be performing the implant surgery on me. His name was Dr. O'Reilly, a big robust Irishman, who seemed to be very knowledgeable in the field of cardiology. He briefed me on what to expect during the biventricular device implant operation, checked my vitals, and patiently answered the many questions that I had. He claimed to be one of the pioneers in heart implant devices and stated that he had performed more surgeries than he cared to remember.

I asked Dr. O'Reilly the question that had been uppermost on my mind. "Since the medications didn't work, what if this device doesn't work either?"

"Well, Deborah, the only option then would be a heart transplant." I gulped. He added that my EKG revealed a deficient left bundle branch block that was wider than any he had ever seen. He told me that in all his experience as a cardiologist, he had never seen a heart as bad as mine. This piece of information was unsettling, to say the least. "However," he said, "ten years ago there would not have been anything we could have done for your type of heart disease. With today's technology, you have an excellent chance of survival. Would you like to see a pacemaker?"

I nodded.

He left the room for a moment and came back with a humongous device that was approximately eight inches long and one and a half inches wide. It must have weighed at least five pounds! I started hyperventilating. I was quick to point out the negative aspects of this device and wondered out loud where they would place it in my small frame. And even if they were able to place it in my chest, it was so huge and clumsy looking. Surely it would slip from wherever it was implanted and possibly puncture other inner organs! Richard tried to reassure me, saying my body would adjust to it and everything would be fine. It was clear to me he was grasping at straws.

As I contemplated grabbing my coat and running from his office, Dr. O'Reilly held out another device that was approximately two by two inches long and no more than a half inch wide. It weighed just a few ounces.

"It's a combination pacemaker and defibrillator," he said. He smiled. "This is the one we use today in biventricular implants, not the one you have in your hand."

I immediately set the larger, older version of the device down and breathed out an air of relief. This smaller mechanical piece was more do-able.

"That older device was what we used to use ten years ago," Dr. O'Reilly said. Because of its size we had to implant it into the patient's abdomen. With today's advancement in the treatment of heart patients, pacemakers have been revolutionized."

He further explained that this device is for heart patients who are also at risk for sudden cardiac death. While functioning like a normal pacemaker to treat slow heart rhythms, it would also deliver small electrical impulses to the left and right ventricles to help them contract at the same time. My echocardiogram revealed that my left and right ventricles were doing their own thing and not working together. When the right and left ventricles are harmoniously synchronized, it allows the heart to pump more efficiently.

The biventricular device has an additional feature that treats dangerously fast heart rhythms that can lead to cardiac arrest. If the device senses heartbeats that are dangerously fast it delivers a shock to the heart. This shock stops the abnormal rhythm that can lead to immediate death. It was this *shock* that terrified me.

Nevertheless, Dr. O'Reilly had made a positive impression on Richard and me, and we were confident that with his level of expertise, the surgery would go well. It was scheduled for March 19th, which gave me enough time to prepare mentally and physically for this next step.

The day of the surgery finally arrived. There were some complications in inserting the biventricular implant devise in my chest. An overnight stay turned into seven days of hospitalization. And one surgery turned into three. Still, the desired outcome was finally accomplished. My heart no longer had to overwork itself to pump blood through my body and my life span has been extended considerably due to modern technology. With the support of my children, but especially Monique, my nurse and caregiver, it seemed that I finally was on the road to recovery and looked forward to a bright future.

CHAPTER 10

Nuttier Than a Fruitcake or Sweeter Than Honey

WITH MY PACEMAKER IMPLANT SURGERY and the worst of my health issues behind me, the rest of 2010 was shaping up to be a pretty good year. Or so I thought.

As soon as I was recovered from the surgeries, I decided it was time to take flight, to implant some vitality into my psyche and pleasure into my life. With my physicians' permission and my family's blessings, I purchased an airline ticket to Freeport, Bahamas.

To me, the Caribbean was the Motherland whose mesmerizing blue ocean and white sandy beaches offered the spiritual and emotional rejuvenation that I so desperately needed. Upon my arrival, my Bahamian brothers and sisters warmly greeted me and provided all the hospitality needed to make my stay in this safe haven most pleasurable. The older women scolded me on a number of occasions for traveling alone. And the men would constantly remind me to slow down when I walked because I seemed so intense.

The resort accommodations at the Radisson Grand Lucayan were most welcoming with a luxurious flair. Thrilled to find that an onsite casino was located in the lower level of the hotel, I reveled in the fact that I could engage in my casino therapy at will. And the many shopping venues located in every direction created a dream come true for a shopaholic such as myself. My favorite market was the Port Lucaya Marketplace where flea and street markets abounded. I could shop to my heart's content, buying articles made by the island natives or commercial items imported from the states.

In my hotel room I perused numerous pamphlets and brochures as I planned my itinerary for the week. To my delight, one of the offerings was horseback riding, an activity I'd had some experience with and loved doing. After settling in, I arranged for transportation to Pinetree Stables. To my delight, I was able to select my own horse. Of course, I selected the creamy-colored Palomino who reminded me of Trigger, the horse from the famous *Roy Rogers* TV show which I had watched frequently as a child. This beauty stood about fifteen hands high with an alluring, flowing mane and tail that would make even Beyoncé jealous. I took my time becoming acquainted with him before the ride by rubbing his neck and softly whispering his name, "*Ashanti*." Hopefully, this method of getting acquainted would make Ashanti think twice before bucking me off of him.

In addition, a private horseback riding guide was assigned to me to lead me through a two-hour tour. His presence was greatly appreciated because I could not even see a trail due to the dense, plush plants and trees that surrounded this breathtaking landscape. We proceeded at a steady pace until we reached the base of a tall mountain where we let the horses drink from a cool running stream. The guide, a native Bahamian, explained the history of the Pinetree horse ranch and the mountainous range with first-hand knowledge and a sincere love of his homeland. His eyes sparkled and danced as he named each plant, tree and waterway on the path. This guided tour winded its way through the endangered Pine Forest, past an awesome castle, through an area of sand dunes until, behold! In front of us was the whitest, sandiest beach I'd ever seen, majestically complimented by the bluest, calmest sea.

Without hesitation the tour guide dug his knees into the neck of his steed and yelled with glee. His horse quickly sprinted then galloped at a full run straight into the welcoming sea. Not wanting to be a party pooper, I immediately followed his lead and kicked Ashanti, loosened the reins, and held on for the most invigorating ride of my life. Familiar with the sea, Ashanti ran full force into the warm, mild waves as I literally screamed with delight. This was my first time riding in the surf and the immediate rush of the experience engulfed my body with an excitement and ecstasy that was indescribable. A healing moment to be sure

Upon my return to Sacramento, I looked forward to celebrating my grandson Jayden's second birthday which was quickly approaching. Monique spared no expense in throwing Jayden lavish and fun-filled birthday parties, and I was right along with her in the planning and the celebrating. As the big day approached that June of 2010, boy, did we go overboard! Monique selected a SpongeBob Squarepants theme for the party. There was not a SpongeBob item left in any store within the greater Sacramento area by time we were through. We purchased a SpongeBob cake, ice cream, bowls, forks and spoons, cups, balloons, decorations, toys, books, sheets, covers, sprinklers, shoes, t-shirts, shorts, hats, instruments, CD's and DVD's. Name it and if it had a Spongebob picture on it, we bought it. We had to laugh at ourselves because we went way over the top! But it was just another expression of Monique's crazy love for her baby. And I reveled in it.

As a young, devoted mother, Monique committed herself to making positive changes in her life. That summer she and Jayden moved in with her brother, "Uncle Richard," in order to save money for a new apartment. She worked as a supervisor at her father's airport bookstores and began making monthly payments for new furniture she'd put on layaway. As a supervisor, she was well-organized, well-respected, and well-liked by her subordinates.

She methodically planned her move to total independence which, she announced, would take place in December. That fall she made a down payment on an apartment in the Natomas area, made the final payments on her furniture, and made daycare arrangements for Jayden. Her future looked bright.

The one thing that distressed Monique during this time was that her best friend Alethea's little boy, Jayce, began experiencing excruciating headaches and irritability. Alethea took him to the doctor and he was diagnosed with a terminal brain tumor. Monique was devastated by this news. She called me to say she felt like she was losing her mind because of Jayce's illness. She loved that little boy. I reassured her that she had to be a pillar of strength for Alethea. And she was. Witnessing my daughter's compassion, her strength, and her ability to take charge of her own personal life was a source of joy for me.

The constant that has always been the center of my life is the love, unity, and show of support from my family. They can be nuttier than a fruitcake or sweeter than honey. The common denominator, though, is the love they continue to show me through life's daunting obstacles. After my run-in with cardiomyopathy, my eyes were open to how fragile life could be and how important family was. Without Monique's loving care and the support of every member of my family I would have never survived the eight surgeries and the rehabilitation period during my illness. But now I had started gaining weight—a good thing—and I became more optimistic about the future; especially doting on my two grandsons.

To show my appreciation to my family for their loving support, I planned our first family reunion. Little did I know it would also be our last one.

July Fourth that summer of 2010 was a Sunday. We decided to make our reunion a two-day gathering over the weekend. On Saturday, my sister Beatrice's family and my family united for a day of fun at Marine World/Africa U.S.A. in Vallejo, California. We watched the Chinese acrobats and the dolphin show, rode rides, played games and truly had a fun-filled day. I delighted in watching Monique from the corner of my eye as she ran around frantically trying to keep up with that little ball of energy, Jayden. At one point, he fell, as toddlers do, and hit his head on the ground. Monique went into her overly protective mode and showered Jayden with affection and attention. Later that night she called me, expressing even more concern about this first knot of many to come that was forming on his head. I reassured her that by icing it and watching him closely, she had fulfilled her motherly duty and everything would be all right.

In the days leading up to and during the family reunion, we produced our Nelson Family Reunion Video. Family members were interviewed and videotaped in various settings to make a video that is now so priceless to me. I think of Richard interviewing his youngest sister. He asked Monique, "Who was the most influential person in your life?" Of course, I was anticipating that her response would reinforce that her Mother rocks! But in fact, something much more serendipitous happened. Monique affectionately responded that her son, Jayden, was the most influential person in her life because he made her want to be a better person. Indeed, becoming that "better person" was something she accomplished in a remarkable way, and in my eyes she was the best mother ever!

An additional video clip of Monique was recorded at the family reunion's culminating event. We'd held a family dinner on Sunday, the Fourth, at my son's beautiful home with enough food and fixin's to feed a kingdom. Afterward, we lit memorial candles and shared stories and family legends of those who had passed before us. Our family was so blessed to be able to honor our first recorded ancestor: our great-great-grandfather Marion Charles Weaver. In 1854, he was the product of an African slave and the master's daughter. Candles were lit in his honor and in honor of my mother Beatrice, my father Harold, Aunt Marcella, Uncle Charles, grandmother, grandfather and friends.

After lighting the candles, Richard videotaped as each person in attendance made closing comments. One of my closet friends, Anna Hackett, and her family attended our celebration. Her youngest son, Sean, was the one who had performed in the production of *Alice in Wonderland* with Monique at their elementary school. At the family memorial, when it came to Sean's turn to offer expressions, he introduced his fiancée who was clearly pregnant with their first child. Monique, in a fashion typical of her humorous nature, loudly objected by saying, "That should have been my baby!" Everyone erupted in laughter. That's how spontaneous and infectious Monique's sense of humor could be.

The video we made was reproduced for every family member. Parts of it were televised upon Monique's tragic death. I still have great difficulty viewing it even today.

In tribute to my amazing family, I wrote the following poem shortly after our reunion.

<u>My Family</u>
(By Deborah Nelson)

When you're down and out with no place to go,
When life lands you a devastating blow,
There's always one group that will definitely respond,
It's your Family as magical as a wand.

The Last Portrait: A Psalm For Monique

Family

The ties of blood run deep through each member's veins,
That taps into our ancestors' strength to face life's pains.
A Family's bond is based on a foundation of Love.
Which will elevate you higher like the wings of a dove.

Family is a kinship like no other
That dwells deep in the hearts and minds of all sisters and brothers.
From sunrise to sunset, there are only two things that I can rely on,
That's my God and my Family and our legacy continues on.
The laughter, the chatter and playing the dozens are family traditions,
As we play games, eat dinner and listen to various musical renditions.

Family is truly one of the greatest gifts from God.
They illuminate our existence like a lightning rod.
Is this unique group perfect in every way?
Hell no, it takes commitment, dedication and love to interact each and every day.

Relationships have to be nurtured in order to grow.
Making deposits into securing their love is the only way to go.
It's been said that nothing worthwhile is easy to attain,
In cultivating positive family bonds, it's the same.
But through thick and thin and heaven and hell on this planet,
I'd rather face the trials and tribulations, successes and challenges with these that I inherit.

The legacy of Family will withstand all time.
With their continued brotherhood and support, I'm feeling fine.
Many times it's painful to love unconditionally,
Because of the fear of losing someone that's so close and thought of dearly.

But death is a part of life we cannot deny.
So treat each other right before we meet our Maker in the sky.
Young people, old people, pass your legacy of Family on,
Before this race we are running is done.
The recycling of life with the birth of a child,
Gives Families a reason to rejoice and go buck wild.

So to my precious Family I wish to say,
That in every situation you have made it a brighter day.
God knew what he was doing when he laid the foundation of Family,
With their love and devotion, you'll never be lonely.

I am so thankful for my immediate and extended family and friends.
Who are dearer to me than words could make them understand.
As we go through yet another opportunity to build faith and character together,
Let's always give God the glory for being our strength and our sovereign Creator.

Family is not a word that I regard lightly,
Let the truth be told, you're the breath that I breathe daily and nightly.
The love that you have showered on me is second to none,

The Last Portrait: A Psalm For Monique

It's as powerful as the love shown when God gave us His Son.
Families treat each other with compassion, dignity and respect,
Because each of you deserve it in retrospect.

I'm thankful for the sibling rivalries, the arguments, dysfunctional behaviors and fights,
And remain in awe and amazement on how quickly we forgive with all of our might.
Our different perspectives and secret competitions keep us at the top of our game,
And no one on the outside better call a Family member out of their name.
Or the wrath of the others will quickly step on their neck,
Because only Family members can criticize Family members and keep them in check.

I'm thankful for the warmth in your eyes and the ability to keep it REAL,
It helps me to stay focused and envision that life can be surreal.
Family is your conscience, that little voice in back of your head,
That distinguishes right from wrong, good from bad; you just never forget what they said.

With Family don't walk on eggshells and develop a durable tough skin,
Because they'll never skirt an issue, that's the way of kin.

F – A – M – I – L – Y
Exalts your spirits and that's no lie.
And when this life is over the Family Connection is never done,
Because they are our welcoming committee when we meet Christ the Son,
Endearing, heart-warming, got your back and more,
Are a few terms to describe the tribe that I love and adore.
It's more than the DNA and the outwardly physical features that we inherently share,
It's the emotions, random acts of kindness and psychological dependence that shows
how much we care.

When I hurt I can see the teardrops on your face,
When I am happy your exaltation fills this place.
When I take my last breathe on my journey to the celestial sky,
My Family is the last face I want to see to say good-bye.
Thank you for the good times, bad times and no times too,
Remember forever and always, I will always love you.

"If we have no peace it is because we have forgotten that we belong to each other."
~ Mother Teresa

The reunion that took place that summer of 2010 was the last time my entire immediate family would ever be together again. The family memorial and candle lighting we held seems so appropriate, yet so surreal to me, because the people we honored were our bloodline, our elder ancestors. But the idea that in just five short months, my youngest daughter Monique would join these deceased family members is unfathomable. The ones we memorialized that day were old or sick, and death was the next natural step in their lives. Monique's death was to be violent, unnatural, and unnecessary at only thirty years old.

CHAPTER 11

The Beginning of the End

I REMEMBER CLEARLY THE APRIL day in 2009 when Monique took Jayden to Fly Cuts & Styles Barbershop to get his first haircut. He was not quite a year old and he was determined not to cooperate with the barber during the cutting process. Jayden cried and Monique had to hold him tight. Later, Monique told me the barber had been patient, calling Jayden, "Little Man." The challenge was worth it because Jayden looked quite handsome in his first fade haircut. Monique took her baby to this same barber for the next two years of his young life.

For the last eight months of her life, Monique and Jayden lived with her brother Richard and his son Rayonne. Monique was able to set aside the money she needed for a bigger apartment and to start saving for Jayden's future. It was also during this time that Jayden and Rayonne bonded closer than brothers. Rayonne adored Jayden and protected him as if he was his own little brother. The love Rayonne showered on his little cousin was beyond his three young years of understanding. And Jayden reciprocated this love by looking up to Rayonne and trying to emulate his every move—the good, the bad and the ugly.

The first of December arrived, however, and Richard—ever the big brother—put out a call to his friends to help him move his little sister's brand new furniture into her brand new apartment in the Natomas area of Sacramento. Monique was ready to start her new life of independence. Everything she had worked for, everything she was planning revolved around giving Jayden the best life that she could.

Even though I was now retired, my first love, education, was never too far off the radar. In October of 2010, I had eagerly accepted the opportunity to attend an educational conference at the Radisson Hotel in Sacramento in an effort to network with educational colleagues. During the evening mixer, I connected with an attractive African-American man named Russell. Russell worked with gang members in the Sacramento community. Fascinated with his dedication to this troubled population, I inquired further into what it was that he actually did with gang members. Did he mentor them? Educate them? Guide them to an alternative way of life? As it turned out, none of these.

Russell shared that he took gang members to weekly target practice so that they could become more proficient in their shooting skills. Confused by his admission, I inquired further how this was addressing the issue of gang violence. He candidly replied that if gang members could shoot better they would kill each other off instead of killing innocent bystanders. I was shocked. His was a particularly disturbing and nonchalant "solution" to gang violence. I thought this man to be despicable and lacking in human compassion on every level.

Now, as I fast-forward to December 14, 2010, I sadly understand the misguided method to his man's madness. And I have to wonder, if the gang members who were engaged in the shoot-out that day in the parking lot of the Fly Cuts & Styles strip mall on Stockton Boulevard were better trained to shoot, would they *not* have taken my *Joy*?

At the same time that Monique was living and working each day for Jayden, a former student of mine, Tyrone Wells, chose to support himself and his three children by selling drugs. At nineteen, Tyrone was a product of his dysfunctional environment and a member of a family that was notoriously connected to Sacramento's G-Mobb Gang in Phoenix Park. Known by his gang buddies as "Easy," Tyrone was the product of generational poverty, generational educational failure and generational gang members. Associated with these negative labels, one would think Tyrone was a monster; but he was not.

At Parkway Elementary School, I had known him as a child yearning to be loved. Never a day at school passed where a positive term of endearment or a hug was not exchanged between the two of us. Unfortunately, school hours were from eight to three. What Tyrone went home to after school each day had more influence in his young, divided life than any tenets taught to him in our school.

The first week of December 2010, Tyrone inadvertently set off a chain of events that would end in tragedy for me. Like he'd done many times before, he engaged in selling marijuana in South Sacramento. But this time it was a member of a rival gang, 22-year-old Matthew McKinney, who contacted Tyrone under the guise of wanting to purchase a bag of weed. Instead, at gunpoint, Matthew robbed Tyrone of $40 in cash, an eighth of an ounce of marijuana, and Tyrone's teeth jewelry—a seventeen hundred dollar gold grill mouthpiece.

Tyrone, angry over being duped, told his half-brother, DeAndre Tanner, about the robbery. Tanner, a leader in the ranks of the G-Mobb Gang, was feared in the hood for his violent behavior and criminal connections. Both brothers were now on the look-out for Matthew McKinney. Lo and behold, a week later they spotted him at a discount store in South Sacramento with a buddy of his. A fistfight broke out in the establishment until the four gang-bangers were pepper-sprayed by the store's security guard. However, during the melee, Tanner managed to pummel Matthew pretty good. This retaliation for the robbery continued to fuel the fire between the rival gangs. After the beating, Matthew McKinney and his brother, 27-year old Michael McKinney, made it known they were gunning for Tanner.

Tuesday, December 14th was Monique's day off from work. It was eleven days until Christmas and she was eager to get her annual holiday pictures taken at the one-hour photo shop on Florin Road. She dressed Jayden in his jeans, a white Sunday shirt, and a red and white Santa's hat. The temperature outside was in the mid-fifties, not uncommon for Sacramento in December; the skies were cloudy and it was breezy with scattered rain falling on and off throughout the day. The strip mall that housed the photo shop proved to be busy with holiday shoppers; a lunch crowd packed nearby restaurants.

Monique had texted me the night prior to remind me about my offer to babysit Jayden after the photo shoot. She would drop him off at four. She'd made plans to meet friends for dinner.

Shortly before noon she loaded him into his car seat in her Chevy Tahoe and drove to the photo shop on Stockton Boulevard. During their session, Monique held Jayden close and flashed her pretty smile while the photographer did his magic with the camera. When they were done, he suggested Monique come back in an hour for the pictures.

Jayden apparently got antsy waiting. Monique took him into the barbershop next door where there was a candy machine that Jayden loved to put quarters into. They greeted all the barbers, bought candy from the machine, and then headed back out to her SUV parked in the lot adjacent to the barbershop. I wonder if she sensed the tension that filled the shop that day?

Not long before Monique and Jayden stopped in at Fly Cuts & Styles, a member of the G-Mobb, Cody Wells, Jr.—an acquaintance of, but no relation to Tyrone Wells—came in. He was in the company of Marquis Pettigrew and Pettigrew's four-year-old son. They had come so Pettigrew could get a haircut. Pettigrew took a seat in the barber's chair and Cody Wells, Jr. pulled up a seat beneath an overhead TV to watch a documentary that was playing about former heavyweight champ Mike Tyson.

Sometime later—perhaps while Monique and Jayden were still there—Matthew McKinney arrived in the barbershop to get a touch up. With him was his older brother Michael. Both men were armed, the older brother with a TEC-9 semi-automatic handgun under his shirt. When the McKinneys spotted Wells and Pettigrew, they immediately began mouthing off to the two G-Mobb men, using profane and threatening language. Cody pulled out his phone. Later he would claim to have called a friend to come get him and

Marquis so they could leave. But his phone records indicated that he had in fact called Ronnie Smith, a 35-year-old member of the G-Mobb, who in turn called DeAndre Tanner. The message had been passed on—the McKinney brothers were on the premises.

Not long after Monique and Jayden had left the barbershop, Tanner arrived, armed. With him was a small contingent of backup, including his cousin Demetrius Tanner and Cameron Taylor. It is unclear who began shooting first, but within minutes bullets were flying in all directions. Cody Wells, Jr. slid toward the rear of the barbershop and snatched up his own .40 caliber handgun, which he kept tucked inside his belt, and fired into the melee. Smith, the man whom Wells had called, pulled up in his car just as the firefight spilled outdoors and into the parking lot—where Monique was buckling Jayden into his car seat. Smith jumped out of his vehicle, ducked behind the trunk of his car, and began shooting blindly toward the barbershop with a .38 special.

By the time the shooting had stopped and the police arrived, upwards of thirty-five rounds had been fired. Some of the bullets struck cars parked throughout the parking lot. One of the barbers, three innocent bystanders, and Cameron Taylor were also hit by bullets, sustaining non-life threatening injuries. DeAndre Tanner, the man who had come looking for a fight, was hit in the chest; he later died of his wounds at the hospital.

The police quickly cordoned off the area surrounding it with yellow crime scene tape. They interviewed witnesses and began marking the spots where bullet casings and discarded weapons were found. That's when one of the investigating officers noticed Monique, still leaning into the back seat of her taupe-colored SUV. He called out to her, but got no answer. He also noticed a single bullet hole through the front, driver's side windshield. Realizing something was wrong, he looked into the car and saw blood dripping from her mouth and nose. He knew immediately that the rage of violence in the parking lot had claimed its most innocent victim.

Typically, police officers would never move a body. That is the coroner's job. But in this case, the officer was surprised to see a toddler sitting in the car seat crying quietly, his mother's body draped protectively over him. It was evident that, when the gunfire started, Monique's maternal instincts had kicked in and she had immediately covered her little boy with her own body to protect him from the barrage of bullets. The mother was dead, but her baby was safe.

The officer lifted my daughter's body out of the car and laid her on the pavement next to the vehicle. Firefighters were on the scene almost immediately and tried to revive her, but to no avail.

Another firefighter climbed into the backseat from the other side and unstrapped Jayden. He lifted him out of the car on the far side so he wouldn't see his mother's lifeless body lying on the ground. Quickly he whisked him away and over to where the fire trucks were parked. He held my crying grandson and comforted him until officials from Child Protective Services arrived.

CHAPTER 12

Fine As Wine

That Tuesday afternoon, December 14th of 2010, I had energetically gone about my routine of volunteering at the Kaiser Permanente hospital until two p.m. I'd taken an elderly patient to the flu station for her vaccinations and had passing conversations with a number of people in the hallways. I remember glancing once at my watch; it was 1 p.m. *Why hadn't I felt anything? I wonder now. Why didn't I have a premonition that my baby girl was in danger?*

When I got home I stretched out on the couch to catch a catnap before the time came to babysit little Jayden. That was when the phone rang. I immediately sensed something was wrong by the way Richard was talking, taking those long breathy pauses before saying something uncomfortable, something awful.

"Mama…something bad has happened…to Monique…something really, really bad…"

"What hospital is she at?" I asked, interrupting his telling of the shooting incident. My mind was racing. I had to go to my baby.

That's when he stated the unthinkable. "I think she's dead, Mama. But no one has confirmed it yet."

Yet. Holding on to that little word *yet* gave my sinking heart a thread of hope. All I could say was, "My poor Baby, my poor Baby!"

"Mama, do you want me to come get you?"

"Yes!" I frantically shouted into the phone.

Before hanging up Richard said that he would call me if he received any more information on Monique's condition.

Darkness seemed to suddenly engulf the room and my body went numb as I sank back onto the couch. I agonized over the wait. When would Richard get here? Would he call again to confirm if Monique was alive or dead? The tears began to fall, prayers fervently prayed.

Within a few minutes, I heard a loud knock at the front door. Thinking it was Richard with reassuring news that this had been a case of mistaken identity, that the facts were inaccurate, or that this was some mean cruel joke because surely my child could not be dead—she was only thirty years old and a mother of a two-year-old child for Christ sake!

I rushed to open the door.

A reporter and cameraman from KOVR/CBS 13 TV News stood on my front steps. In shock, I just stared at them. I will never forget the life-shattering words that came out of the reporter's mouth. "Are you Monique Nelson's mother?" I nodded. "I am so sorry for your loss, ma'am."

My breath caught in my throat. *What damn loss?* This is some kind of mistake. As my new reality sank in, I slammed the door, screaming and crying uncontrollably.

Then it started! One huge *thud* near my heart. Then, oh my God, another one. It felt like two mules kicking me in the chest. I started to see stars and began to hyperventilate. Grabbing my chest, I realized this intrusive episode was the defibrillator for my heart condition firing like angry cannons. Dizzy with pain, I felt it fire again. I dropped to my knees as my cell phone began to ring.

Luckily the newsmen had remained at the front door. They heard the commotion from within my living room. He knocked again and asked loudly, "Are you all right?"

I emphatically replied that I was not. I crawled to the front door to let him in. My breath was fading, and that damn defibrillator fired one more time. The newsmen immediately called 911. They relayed my symptoms to the dispatcher and encouraged me to hold on. Somehow I was able to explain that I had cardiomyopathy and that the defibrillator was responding to my accelerated heartbeat.

Within minutes, the first responders were in my living room asking numerous questions and then *boom! boom!* I was shocked two more times.

I was convinced that this life-saving device was going to kill me. I tried not moving to slow the pacing of my heart. Thoughts raced through my mind about what had happened to Monique. Then my thoughts quickly shifted to how thankful I was to be dying so I could catch up with my daughter, because the thought of living without her was unbearable.

Prior to the paramedics placing me on the gurney, I grabbed a picture of Monique and held it close to my heart. I remember feeling a light rain falling as they placed me into the ambulance. As they rushed me to the hospital, I reflected on how just a couple of years ago our whole family was so elated and excited about Monique's new addition to our family, Jayden. Our legacy had been growing as a loving family unit. How did we get to this horrific point in life in just two short years? So much left unsaid. So much left undone.

At the hospital the doctors had to reprogram my defibrillator, stopping the false firing of the device. They reassured me that I wasn't in cardiac arrest, but was understandably traumatized with the knowledge of my daughter's death. My thoughts immediately shifted to my grandson. At this point, I still had no knowledge of what had transpired that resulted in Monique's death. Was Jayden dead too?

I remembered that a longtime friend of the family, Erica Randall, was a police officer. I contacted her and frantically asked for her help. Officer Randall did some checking and told me that Child Protective Services had taken Jayden. The thought of this scenario further devastated me. I told her that Jayden had lost his mother but still had a very involved family and asked her to please find out how we could get him released to us immediately. She agreed to assist us and said she would do all she could to have Jayden released from Child Protective Services.

That evening I was discharged from the hospital. Friends and family congregated at my home; bits of information started trickling in. The media blasted the story of our tragedy on all of the news stations. I couldn't process this information yet; it was too distressing and upsetting to me. So someone took the initiative to unplug the television set in my bedroom.

Later that night, a police officer brought Jayden home to us, and it was clearly evident to me that the baby was confused and possibly in shock. We held him and tried to act as normal—if there is any normality in this kind of situation—as possible. We hugged a little tighter, kissed a little longer, and closely examined Jayden's eyes looking for answers to our many questions. He was the only person to witness Monique's last breath and last moments. Did she say anything? Was she in pain? But the baby could not provide answers. We did not mention Monique for fear of upsetting him. We were terribly fearful of what memories may be flowing through his innocent young mind. All we could do was to remain present in the moment, supporting and comforting each other during this insane time.

My family transformed my guest room into a bedroom for Jayden and placed him down for the evening. Within the hour, he had diarrhea and had to be bathed and his bedding changed. This was his only outward side effect of a day of violence that had to have been etched into his young consciousness for life. This would be the beginning of many sleepless nights for all of us.

The next morning, my sister Beatrice brought the morning newspaper to my bedside. There on the front page of the Sacramento Bee was an image that would haunt me for the rest of my life. Lying next to her Chevy Tahoe was my child's lifeless body, positioned on the cold hard ground with a yellow tarpaulin covering her. Yellow police tape cordoned the crime scene area; an officer was photographed in the process of examining Monique's vehicle. The caption under the picture read: "Responders inspect a bullet hole in the windshield of an SUV belonging to the woman killed Tuesday outside a barbershop on Stockton Boulevard."

That *woman* was my baby. And I was not there for her. During her last moments of life, I was not there for my Monique to hold her, to comfort her, to reassure her that we will see each other again and, most importantly, to take that bullet for her. I was in the hospital while Monique lay alone and very still on that cold, lonely spot for hours and hours. Guilt flooded me as I viewed the newspaper photo. The motivational author, Gretchen

Rubin, famously said that negative feelings like guilt have an important role to play in a happy life. "Guilt is a big flashing sign that something needs to change." Change was certainly on the horizon for me, but the jury is still out on the "happy life" part.

Then to add salt to the wound, a second photo in the newspaper depicted a firefighter holding my two-year-old grandson. Jayden looked remarkably calm and oblivious to the fact that his mother had just paid the ultimate sacrifice. Appreciation filled my heart for the compassion and kindness this firefighter showed my grandson in this dark, dark moment. But how I wished it had been me holding that little boy.

Richard was assigned the bleak task of retrieving his sister's SUV from the barbershop parking lot. I watched him pick up the vehicle on the evening news. The lonely drive was televised and narrated by news reporters in the greater Sacramento area. The single bullet, which crashed through Monique's windshield and pierced her heart created a splintered hole that blocked his vision as he slowly drove the SUV to his home. Most people like to avoid difficult situations. My son faced this painful obstacle with reverence and out of love for his baby sister. To see the strength he portrayed in completing this task broke my heart but made this mother proud.

Although he appeared to be in total control of his emotions and the situation, deep down inside I knew the truth. Monique was his baby sister. She'd lived with him for the past year. They'd raised their children together and were thick as thieves. Because I was a single parent, many times Richard had to play the father's role to his younger siblings. He faithfully made gestures to boost Monique's self-esteem during her formative years. He would tell her how pretty she was. How cool she was. Monique's face would beam with a love and pride that was reserved only for her big brother. To make this final ride had to be devastating for my son.

After Monique's death, Tamora, Richard and I scrambled to get our bearings. We filled our days with planning Monique's funeral arrangements, cleaning out her apartment, taking care of Jayden, and thinking ahead to how we would formalize his living arrangements within our family. It is amazing how the body can operate on autopilot while the cognitive ability is on shutdown. We were so engulfed in shock that even today family members are vague on exactly who did what and when. But staying busy is the best friend to the grieving. So that is exactly what we did.

I didn't know how I was going to get through the funeral arrangements. Beatrice had lost her husband, Richard Bailey, four years before to lung cancer. Following his death, she wrote and published a highly acclaimed self-help book title, *Farewell, My Friend: A Step-By-Step Guide To Handling a Serious Illness and Even the Death of a Loved One* (2008). Besides her own personal experience, Beatrice is a motivational speaker and bereavement lecturer with a degree in psychology. Her expertise was our saving grace as we planned the Homegoing Celebration for Monique. Those who have spent their spiritual lives in the African-American Christian tradition will understand that a Homegoing Celebration is vibrant in nature. We celebrate the life of our loved one and rejoice in knowing that they are now safe in the arms of our Lord and Savior, Jesus Christ. Beatrice was instrumental in dealing with the logistics of designing and publishing the Homegoing Celebration programs, dealing with the church arrangements, and managing the crowds.

Monique's father Richard, her brother Richard, Tamora and I collaborated on the funeral arrangements. We chose the Thompson Funeral Home because her father already had a relationship with them. He had used them to help bury his brothers a few years earlier. Ironically just several months before, Monique had accompanied me to another funeral home. When I was in the throes of dealing with my many heart issues, it occurred to me that I needed to be prepared in the event of my own sudden demise so that my family wouldn't have to bear the burden of paying for my funeral expenses. Monique, ever the caregiver, drove me to the Morgan Jones Funeral Home to inquire about my funeral arrangements. She and I met with one of the representatives to get an estimate for my eventual burial. Monique asked for a brochure for herself; she was interested not so much to take care of her own end-of-life business as it was for Jayden's welfare. And now here I was at the Thompson Funeral Home, this time inexplicably taking care of business for her. The casket we chose was simple, but elegant; a pale lilac in color.

After meeting with the funeral director, Tamora and Beatrice accompanied me as I performed the heart-breaking task of buying my youngest child a burial dress. Monique had always teased me about my lack of taste when it came to buying her clothes. "Mama, you dress me like we are in the '70's," she would say.

The three of us ached with dread as we looked at a number of outfits, wanting Monique to look her best in her lilac casket. The flowers we had planned would have a lilac color in them as well. With that in mind, we agreed upon a deep orchid, almost wine-colored dress made of satin and lace. I wanted to give my baby girl something of mine to take with her. I asked that my favorite rhinestone-collared necklace be placed around her neck to accessorize her outfit.

I reminisced about the many occasions the ladies in our family had to dress up: for family weddings, parties, etc. It was always so much fun! Dressing your child for her Homegoing Celebration, well, there are just no words to describe it. Especially because, as a parent, the natural process of life is that your child is supposed to bury you, not vice versa.

Cleaning out Monique's apartment was an eerie, uncanny experience. She had moved in and purchased new furniture just two weeks before her death. I felt a mother's pride as I entered my daughter's immaculate abode. Jayden's room was decorated in a little boy's fashion with action figure toys, a child's leather chair with a matching piano, and all the brightness and hope of a happy future manifested throughout the room. Monique's living room was decorated with flowers, family pictures, and black leather furniture like I had in my first apartment. When Monique was a young girl growing up, most of our disagreements were over cleaning the house. Now I could plainly see that my little girl had transformed into a responsible, conscientious mother.

When I finally brought myself to enter her bedroom that first time after her death, I smelled each of her pieces of clothing in the closet and in the drawer. I never wanted to forget her fragrance, the total essence of Monique.

With heavy hearts we bagged all of her belongings to donate to Goodwill, setting aside a few personal keepsakes. From somewhere deep within my soul a rage rose up; I began to scream and holler at the top of my lungs. I cursed the demons that murdered my baby. I even cursed God for forsaking us. What happened to that guardian angel that each of us were supposed to have? What happened to the promises of the righteous? My daughter loved God. Why didn't *He* save her? My anger and grief devoured my soul.

Richard took me outside and made me walk around until I calmed down. We finished our arduous task and, like Monique, her beautiful apartment was no more.

At one point we were meeting with an attorney to seek guidance on how to obtain permanent custody of Jayden. During this meeting, Richard revealed something he'd discovered that we found to be somewhat mystical in nature. He had cleaned Monique's SUV and in the backseat he found a handwritten will and testament prepared by my daughter. Her last written request was basically a blueprint on how she wanted her son, Jayden, raised in the unlikely event of her death. It also included her burial wishes and where to find her finances.

This document was as much a shock to me as it was an enigma. Why was it in the back of Monique's vehicle? When did she write it? Why would a healthy thirty-year-old woman be planning for her death? Did Monique have a premonition that something was going to happen to her? We always said she was an "old soul," someone who had been here before. I flashed back to that day in my bedroom when she had backed up against the wall, saying, "Mama, sometimes the child goes before the parent."

In her will Monique had stipulated that, if she passed before the date of July 6, 2011 any money received from her insurance company should go toward her funeral arrangements. She wished to be cremated. She even stated the dollar cost of various funeral services based on the brochure, I assume, from Morgan's Funeral Home. If she passed after the July date, she conceded, the family could determine whether she should be cremated or buried, but if buried she wanted her casket to be purchased from Walmart to save money, so that the rest of what she had could go to Jayden. "If viewing of the body is the way you choose to go, make sure I'm *fine as wine*," she instructed, requesting that we play the gospel song "I'm Safe In His Arms."

Monique was determined that Jayden's savings account not be touched, even by him, until he was of an appropriate age, and even then with limits. This and some additional personal information were reflected in her last will and testament.

"Any personal belongings," she'd also written, "can be sold or given away to the poor." Then she went on to state, "It is MANDATORY that in Jayden's room he has a BIG picture of me and him by his bedside. And every day you tell him how much mommy loved him and there's no greater joy than to have him as my son. I ask that you treat him as he was your own son and give him all the love that he needs. Explain to him that death comes to us all. It's the end of one life, but the beginning of another…Of course my prayer is I grow old with my son or just to see him become a man but we just never know what tomorrow holds. So I'd rather be prepared…" She further expressed her desire that in the event of her demise, Jayden stay with her side of the family. And that, "College is a MUST!"

Every time I read this document, chills run up and down my spine. Monique had premonitions that something was going to happen to her. Out of the blue, when she was alive, she would ask her brother and sister to promise to take care of Jayden in case anything happened to her. We would just laugh it off as one of her ridiculous superstitions, but inwardly I felt very uncomfortable about the possibilities. Monique used to tell me that she felt like she was clairvoyant. I would look at her in amazement and listen to her reasons why she felt she had this special talent. Her grandmother, my mother, Beatrice Hamer Toney, had this gift. Like Monique, she made predictions about her death, such as the prediction that it would rain on the day she was buried. Indeed, it did! Monique and I talked about Nostradamus' predictions about the world ending in the year 2000. Little did we know at that time that our world would be ending, as we knew it, in 2010.

The words in her last will and testament put me in awe of the human spirit and the infinite, intriguing knowledge it possesses. Does our spirit know when we are going to die? Do we then act accordingly?

After reading Monique's wishes for her burial in her will, we quickly altered her funeral arrangements as instructed. Unknowingly, we had already chosen to dress her in a wine-colored dress and, strange as it may sound, I knew she would be *fine as wine*.

Next, we found a gospel soloist to sing her favorite song, "Safe In His Arms!" Oddly enough, I used to listen to that song after my father's funeral in 1983. Monique could not have known this because she was only three years old at the time. Who knows? Maybe she *was* clairvoyant.

On Thursday, December 23, 2010, I buried my lifeline, Monique Roxanne Nelson. But she was not in that casket alone. A major part of me was buried with her. If it had not been for my family and my grandson, I fear to think of what I would have done to myself afterward.

Over a thousand people attended Monique's Homegoing Celebration at St. Paul Missionary Baptist Church in Oak Park. Along with immediate family members, relatives, friends, and her co-workers from the bookstore, numerous members of the Sacramento community turned out to honor and say goodbye to my daughter. Members of the City Council, including Holly Benet (who has since retired from the Council) and members of the Sacramento City Unified School Board of Directors, including then Board member James Tucker (now a City Councilman) were present, as were members of the area Chamber of Commerce and Law Enforcement including Chaplin Eric Moss.

We chose not to bring Jayden to his mother's funeral. He was simply too young to comprehend it. The viewing of the body continues to frighten me. I couldn't risk what viewing Monique's deceased body might do to Jayden's psyche. I wanted him to remember Monique when she was still alive and vibrant. Not still and cold. We would make sure he had plenty of opportunities to experience the photographs, videos, and memorabilia in future days and years.

As much as I dreaded seeing her that way, I will never forget how beautiful Monique looked laying there in her open casket, wearing the deep purple dress we'd picked out, her long hair draping her shoulders. *Fine as wine.* She seemed so peaceful, one hand folded over the other. Disappointingly, the necklace I had given her as my final gift was not visible, due to her positioning. But I knew she was wearing it. There was comfort in that. The last portrait of Monique and Jayden was enlarged and displayed in oversized frames on each side of the casket.

The Reverend Isaiah McDowell delivered a most spiritual eulogy. Afterward, somehow, I found the strength to share what was in my heart. When I finished, Monique's father, Richard, spoke.

And finally, Monique's brother Richard stood and recounted his many happy childhood memories of his sister. He reflected on Monique's mischievous and daredevil nature, even sharing about the time her head had become wedged between the bars of the iron gate and how the postman and I had to free her by applying butter and Crisco all over her head and ears. That elicited quite a few chuckles from among her mourners. He also spoke about how spiritual Monique was, how we had discovered books on religion and Scripture verses all over her apartment when we were cleaning it out. And of course he told the mourners she had chosen the song "Safe In His Arms" for this melancholy service.

As difficult as it was, everyone brought their strongest face and honored a classy Lady in a classy fashion. That's not to say that tears weren't shed. Au contraire, a river of tears were shed inside the church and out, but in a respectful manner for the family.

My sister Ellouise could not be there, but she sent a loving tribute from her family in Davenport, Iowa to be read:

Monique Roxanne Nelson
(By Ellouise Clayvon)

A dearly loved Daughter
A dearly love Sister
A dearly loved Granddaughter
A dearly loved Niece
A dearly loved Aunt
A dearly loved Friend
A dearly loved Cousin
A dearly loved person all around.
Dearly loved by all who knew and cared for her!
The above will never define what Monique meant to people. She was and is so much more than just words. She is an un-destroyable loving energy that remains with us eternally.
Bound by the chains of our hearts, our memories and our love.
A pillar of light and joy to both planes of existence.
Now her work continues in spirit, where she is tenderly embraced by the ultimate "truth"
of life and the great love of Divine spirit.
Forever with and watching over you. Those left behind have suffered a tragic physical
loss, but gained a love so raw and pure that now sees no restriction or burden of the shell we call the physical body.
Many say "Goodbye" while she says, "I'm Home."
Closer to us now than she ever was on earth's plane…her spirit roams free…to be where it is needed. Never far from our side and present with every loving thought.
We grieve now, not for her, but for our own physical loss.
As we work through our own personal inner journeys of grief, Monique will suspend us

The Last Portrait: A Psalm For Monique

in love and divine light. So that we can carry on in life,
with love in our hearts and compassion at our core.
You are life. You are love.
"Let it be" are your words from spirit.
You will teach many of us to love more, to live more, to not worry about the small stuff,
to take more risks in life, to capture happiness in our hands and hold it tight…
but most of all you will teach us to "Let it Be."
We love you always and forever.
 ~ Aunt Ellousie, Uncle Joe, Little Joe, Dominica and Andrea Clayvon Klan

The memorial service lasted nearly two hours. The images in the touching slideshow montage of Monique's life brought back the fondest of memories for family and friends. The Scripture readings and the benediction are pretty much a blur. But the gospel music and the prayers rising to heaven on behalf of my baby are forever seared into my heart. My own prayer was that the service pleased Monique and that she could witness the impact her young life had made on all in attendance. Monique was a heroine who sacrificed her life for her son. Her Homegoing Celebration was befitting of the Queen that she was and a psalm of praise to the life she lived.

When the service was concluded and her casket rolled back out of the church and set in front of the black limousine hearse, white doves were released into the hazy December sky to personify Monique's soul returning peacefully to the heavens. Then a multitude of cars proceeded to Camellia Memorial Lawn Cemetery to place my youngest daughter in a mausoleum that faces the sun each morning.

I simply could not place her in the ground. Witnessing many of my ancestors and associates buried in that traditional fashion reminded me of the insurmountable dread I'd feel each time I visited their graves. My thinking was I would not place my baby in that worm-infested ground. And I couldn't allow her body to be burned, even though she had requested that in her will (likely as a cost-saving measure). In addition, I had purchased my burial site within the same tomb so I could be with Monique for eternity. I may pay for my hubris in the afterlife, though. I can hear Monique complaining, *"Oh damn, I just can't get away from her!"* with that smile that will live on in my memory forever.

Let the truth be told, it's no more consoling to visit my deceased child in a mausoleum above ground as opposed to being buried six feet under. It's all painful because a child's death is always premature. A child is supposed to bury the parent. It's an anomaly for the parent to bury their child.

The one person in Monique's life who did not attend her funeral was Kenyatta Butler, Jayden's biological father. We weren't surprised. We hadn't seen anything of him for nearly two years—since shortly after Jayden was born. Monique and Kenyatta had parted ways amicably; he had moved out of town and basically out of our lives.

But just weeks after Monique's funeral, Kenyatta was back in our lives. And he was demanding his son. Could we possibly lose two of our most cherished family members, Monique *and* Jayden, within a month's time? The Nelson family was terrified by this unnerving prospect.

CHAPTER 13

A Clean-Cut Case

THE SACRAMENTO COMMUNITY WAS STUNNED by Monique's death. The carnage that took place at the Fly Cuts & Styles Barbershop on December 14, 2010 sparked an outcry from the local chapter of the NAACP, local politicians, activists, ministers, police officers, family and friends. Candle light vigils, prayer meetings, Facebook, blogs, and press conferences were active in expressing their sympathy for what had happened in the community. The massive media coverage and chants at rally sites exploded with slogans such as "Enough is Enough!" and "Stop the Violence!"

There were repeated pleas to crackdown on the increasing chaos in the streets of Sacramento. Community leaders called for unity and asked all citizens to take personal responsibility for protecting the neighborhoods in which they resided. Unfortunately, there is a strange code of conduct within the Black community. Snitching to the police is considered a more serious infraction than the felonious act committed. Police were challenged with getting witnesses to step up and provide the needed information in order to apprehend the criminals responsible for Monique's death. Sacramento County Sheriff's Sgt. Tina Cooper told the press that there were about two dozen people playing games in the back room of the barbershop when the gunfight broke out. Police investigators managed to interview at least twenty of them, but nobody was willing to cooperate or say much of anything for fear of retaliation.

Bullets had hit both DeAndre Tanner and Cameron Taylor during the melee and both were immediately taken to a local hospital. Tanner died of his wounds following surgery. Taylor, whose wounds were non-life threatening, was arrested.

Michael McKinney was taken into custody two days after the shootout. The California Highway Patrol stopped the car in which he was riding on Interstate 5 near a stretch of highway called The Grapevine just north of Los Angeles. Two women in the car with him at the time were questioned, but released a short time later.

Within the next month Matthew McKinney, Demetrius Tanner, and Ronnie Smith were all arrested. Cody Wells, Jr., however, was still on the run, considered to be armed and dangerous. A manhunt was on and the Sacramento County Sheriff's Department posted a reward of a thousand dollars.

Ballistics testing done during the forensics investigation revealed that it was a bullet from Ronnie Smith's gun that had pierced Monique's heart. On February 11, 2011 murder, weapons, and assault charges were filed against all five men, as well as against the fugitive, Cody Wells, Jr.

The outpouring of support for Jayden after the violent death of his mother was extremely considerate and altruistic in nature. Several restaurants and organizations held donation drives. Over a hundred gifts addressed to Jayden were delivered to Richard's house on Christmas Eve—everything from a Hot Wheels bike to bath toys.

"It just touched my heart to know these people are coming together to support Jayden," Richard said to the news media.

Total strangers had donated gifts so that our little boy could have a "happy" Christmas. Of course, there was no joy to be had that day. Jayden loved his new toys, but what he really wanted was his mother. He didn't understand that she was gone, that he would never see her again.

That first Christmas, just two days after Monique's burial, was so incredibly surreal it did not even seem possible. My foolish goal was to strive for some level of normalcy for an abnormal occasion. I cooked all of Monique's favorite meals and Jayden had two rooms full of toys and gifts from the well-wishers.

The Last Portrait: A Psalm For Monique

Richard and his family, Tamora, and my children's father Richard senior were all gathered. Everyone tried to be as upbeat and merry as possible for the children. No one mentioned the obvious, the "elephant in the room."

But, as Jayden and Rayonne opened their gifts and I was setting the table, Monique's father suddenly stood up and announced, "I can't take this," and abruptly left. I was shocked and disappointed. Once again, I felt, my surviving children and I had to be the glue to make this family stick together. It was a nice try, the attempt to keep Christmas "merry" that day, but the fact of the matter is neither Christmas nor any traditional holiday will ever be the same without Monique. I so desperately miss hearing her say, "You did a good job, Mom!"

The months after Monique's death were extremely difficult for me; but Jayden was only two years old, and so his coping skills were much better than mine. To my mind, it was a double-edged sword. On the one hand, it was a great relief that he expressed no understanding of the violent tragedy that he had survived. But on the other hand, as time progressed, he remembered less and less of the woman who gave and saved his life.

In the beginning, he would awaken or at sporadic times throughout the day he would call for Mama and even cry. But the more telling moments were when he was silent and just peering out the window or staring into space with a void expression. I would infer that this reflective moment was some remembrance of the past, so I would make him stay as busy as I was: playing, coloring, singing, watching movies and regularly going to the bounce house. Periodically, I would show him pictures of Monique and tell him real life stories about his mother's life and love for him. He would smile, but his level of understanding of what had happened was vague. As adults, we were dealing with this tragedy with denial, avoidance and anger; and so, struggling to know how to properly handle Jayden's loss, I found the need to seek professional help.

The child psychiatrist we met with advised, "Just be honest and answer any questions that he may ask, but don't push the subject matter on him." He shared his opinion that Jayden was too young to remember the event; but in my heart I believed that we really did not know what was in Jayden's subconscious mind. He understood fear. He understood that Mommy was hurt. Just because he did not have the verbal skills to express it doesn't mean he didn't understand that something was very wrong. The doctor also stated that when Jayden was ready to know more, he would let us know.

You know the old cliché, "When it rains it pours?" After the tragedy, we had a storm of issues to deal with. In the week between Monique's death and her burial, Kenyatta Butler, Jayden's father, had learned about what happened through social media. At the same time, news reporters contacted him. They had tracked him down, interviewed him, and aired the interview on television. Then we learned, via Facebook, that Kenyatta and his girlfriend, Keley Nicole Johnson, had plans to gain custody of Jayden.

I was shell-shocked. How could this be? I had met Kenyatta when he was dating my daughter. Once she became pregnant, I never saw him again until the day Jayden was born. And then, not again after that. Monique rarely spoke of Jayden's father except to say that he had moved on and was no longer in their life. And of course, I had never met Keley. How could they now say they had a right to my grandson?

How quickly our family situation seemed to go from bad to worse. Not only were we trying to gain our bearings after losing our beloved Monique, but we were suddenly forced to deal with people we did not know and did not have a relationship with. And in our view, they appeared relentless during a time we were trying to find solace. These people were tugging at our fragile heartstrings with the threat of causing us to lose another family member. In my mind, they were taking my purpose for living and literally demolishing my last stronghold for the institution of my family.

So when this young man came to town in January of 2011—just weeks after we had buried Monique—to claim his son, I totally freaked out. We did not have a relationship with him, I reminded everybody. He had been absent from Monique's and Jayden's lives; and one of Monique's written requests in her last will and testament stipulated, "You must do your best to keep Jayden with my side of the family."

Jayden and I had always enjoyed a unique grandmother/grandson relationship even prior to Monique's death. She would frequently comment, "Just look at you two!" The day of Jayden's birth I held him and gave him his first bottle, and from that first moment I knew I was hooked for life.

Now, two and a half years later, my family was united in grief and in the desire to keep Jayden within the family unit that had raised and loved him for the first years of his life. After all, he was the only connection that we had to my deceased daughter, the love of our life. I was ready to do battle with Kenyatta Butler.

I immediately filed a petition seeking guardianship of my grandson. To my relief I was granted temporary guardianship with custodial rights until an investigation and the mediation process between Kenyatta and myself could be completed. With the family's blessing and support, I became Jayden's primary caregiver.

Per Monique's final request, I enrolled him in a private Christian School called the Capital Christian Center. Donations and Monique's Social Security check enabled us to pay his monthly tuition. To provide me with breaks, my former daughter-in-law, Karen Nelson, kept Jayden on the weekends where his relationship continued to flourish with his cousin, Rayonne. Richard devotedly included Jayden on all family outings and in activities with Rayonne. Jayden's grandfather, Richard senior, visited his grandson on a weekly basis. And Tamora regularly sent money for him from Los Angeles.

Jayden's presence in my home kept me sane, kept me busy, and kept me immersed in love. Which was a good thing, because the custody proceedings were like a dagger in my heart. Fighting everyone from court-appointed personnel, to the lawyers, judges, and Kenyatta just exacerbated my grieving, my anger and my growing sense of hopelessness and helplessness. We had done nothing wrong, my family and I, except to stand up for my murdered daughter. However, we were paying the heaviest of dues. I was being analyzed, dissected and even demonized by some of the people in the system. My health came into question, even though my doctor gave me a clean bill of health.

I was told by one lawyer I'd hired that "this is going to be a clean-cut case," and that the best place for consistency for the child was "with the only family he has known for his young two years." A court-appointed mediator interviewed me and visited our home and Jayden's school. She assured me she would recommend our home for Jayden. However, when she met with another court-appointed counselor, the mediator changed her recommendation for placement. This counselor did not like my response to her question, "What will you do to insure Kenyatta visits Jayden?" In my mind, I did not think that was my responsibility. Therefore, I responded "Nothing!" Wrong answer! Unfortunately, Monique had not gotten her will notarized, nor had she filed it with an attorney; therefore court officials would not honor her final request for Jayden to remain with her family.

A lot of fighting, court costs, and deeper feelings of loss took place as we strove to keep Jayden with us. After a several-months-long battle—despite what had transpired between Monique, Jayden, and his father in the past, or the extenuating circumstances as to how Jayden had become motherless—in May of 2011 the court awarded custody of Jayden to his biological father. Our family was awarded visitation rights every other weekend, and I was assigned guardianship over Jayden's estate, of which there was none.

For me, that day, I suffered a second bullet to the heart.

Anger once again dominated my psyche. "Haven't we suffered enough?" I cried. I was starting to feel like Job; plagued with one challenge after another.

The weight of the world was on my shoulders as I slowly packed all of Jayden's belongings. He would be living in La Verne in Southern California with his new family. I will say Kenyatta had been committed to commuting to see his son regularly during the time of the custody battle. That was when we knew he was serious about assuming responsibility for his son.

Jayden naturally experienced some confusion during this time. Here I was trying to quickly establish some stability in his shattered life after his mother's death, and his father was pulling in another direction. I had assumed Monique's role, and like her I made sure that everything in my life was about Jayden. There was such a special love, a special bond between that child and me. Every mistake that I had made with Monique, I was determined not to do again with Jayden. But this second chance was not to be.

Jayden had responded well to his first meeting with his father in January. I shouldn't have been surprised. He has always been a very respectful child and he gets along well with all people. At Chuck E. Cheese's, his favorite restaurant, he always made friends instantly and would embrace passers-by as his buddies. Monique had been the same way. Her friends meant the world to her. We had arranged for father and son to meet at Richard's home. Kenyatta brought Keley and her two children.

In hindsight, we consider it a blessing that Jayden's transition was smooth because he had been through so much in his young life. By having children for Jayden to play with was a big plus in their reunion. The adjustment was less kind to me, because Jayden was the center of my joy and pain. He was the lifeline to my deceased daughter. But once again, we had to let go and Let God!

When the time came to turn him over to his father permanently, I dropped him off at the California Expo grounds in the company of Rayonne's mother Karen, because I could not bear to see the exchange.

I was so devastated by this new loss that I literally became bedridden for two weeks. A river of tears flowed. I had failed Monique once again, I believed. Control is an illusion—this is the greatest lesson learned during this tumultuous time. I was totally powerless to stop my precious Jayden from moving over four hundred miles away from his maternal family and friends—from me. I was terrified of the lifestyle that he might be entered into, because all I knew of his father were stories that were swirling around, stories that weren't necessarily positive.

But I did not know Kenyatta. I did not know the truth about him. I underestimated his love for his son. For this man and his love of Jayden, I eventually learned gratitude.

The custody battle that took place in family court that first year after Monique died was a horrific ordeal for me. Maybe it was preparing me for the forthcoming nightmare in the criminal justice system.

CHAPTER 14

The Rippling Effects of Street Violence

SPRING ARRIVED AND THERE STILL had been no arrest of the sixth and final suspect in Monique's killing—Cody Wells, Jr. In early April of 2011 the TV show *America's Most Wanted* stepped in to help publicize the case. Starring missing-children's advocate John Walsh, a segment of the popular television show focused on a reenactment of the events that happened on that awful December day inside and outside of Fly Cuts & Styles Barbershop. The suspect that was still missing was thought to be responsible for calling the rival gang to the scene and for shooting his gun from within the barbershop. The TV show's description of him was thorough and frightening. He had an extensive set of tattoos covering his torso, including the words "Only God Should Judge" on his upper left bicep, the words "4th Avenue" on his upper back, and a gun stenciled onto his stomach as if tucked into his waistband.

I believe that the *America's Most Wanted* TV program was a crucial agent in the arrest of Wells in mid-April. He had apparently fled to Washington State immediately after the shootout, but eventually returned to the Sacramento area. Detectives from the Sheriff's Major Crimes Bureau and Gang Suppression Unit located him at a Sacramento County residence and took him into custody without incident.

The threat of street violence in the U.S. holds millions of people captive and fearful in their homes and communities large and small. America is "the land of the free," but due to crime and the availability of firearms, it seems that America has become a country free to shoot at will. It seems to me that our youth do not know the difference between reality and fantasy with all the violence they see on television and experience through video games. In their world if someone is shot, that person will return on the next week's episode or the game starts over. It doesn't occur to many young people that death is permanent, and that the damage caused to the victim's family and friends has life-long ramifications.

It seems that some violent people are without remorse or fear of the consequences for their behavior. I am aware of numerous programs aimed at reducing street violence across the nation. However, their results have been minimal. As long as the statistics on street violence continue to grow, as long as another son becomes motherless or a mother loses her child to the firepower on the streets, not one person can be satisfied with the effort so far.

The level of violence of all kinds throughout the world is simply mind-boggling. I cannot turn on the television, read a newspaper, surf the Internet or listen to the radio without being informed about a homicide, suicide, an act of terrorism or mass murder. My level of awareness has become heightened due to our own experience with Monique's tragedy. I am consumed by all the needless and senseless deaths that have taken place in my lifetime: the twenty children and six staff killed at Sandy Hook Elementary (two years to the day after my own daughter was murdered), Trayvon Martin, Marvin Gaye, Michael Brown, Biggie Smalls, Tupac, Tamir Rice, the Columbine students, the victims of the Colorado theater massacre, the thirty-two college students at Virginia Tech, the forty-nine killed in an Orlando night club, the one hundred and forty five Pakistani school children killed by the Taliban, the three thousand World Trade Center victims, and my own Monique Roxanne Nelson. The list is so incredibly vast and continues to grow each day.

Are we a society overwhelmed with mental health issues? With loss of spirituality? The breakdown of the family unit? Media brainwashing and other social issues that contribute to a violent nature? We know the causes; but what is the answer to quell the level of violence in this world so our children and our children's children can thrive in a safe environment? These were the questions that consumed me in the days, weeks, and months following Monique's death by gunfire—and still plague me to this day.

And on top of it all, the television inundates the public with series, both fiction and non-fiction, such as CSI, Forensic Files, Criminal Minds, Dateline, Swamp Murders, I Killed My BFF, Kendra: Homicide Hunter, and the list goes on and on. A world with this kind of mindset, a fascination for violence and murder, truly brings into focus the state of our moral compass.

I must confess, though; I do watch these real-life stories. Some may think me strange that I watch homicide mysteries but there is a method to my madness. First, parents who have had a child murdered do not always have a lot of people they can talk to about the experience. I wanted to learn how families, especially mothers, survived the homicide of their child. I wanted to learn how the justice system worked and how much evidence is needed for a guilty verdict. I wanted to learn if there was life after grief. The mothers interviewed on these programs validated some of my most personal thoughts. I knew there would be no *real* justice for my murdered child. Even if the culprit gets the death penalty, it cannot bring my loved one back. I can only try to insure that this criminal does not have the opportunity to kill again. Second, I will never get over the loss of my child. I may go on. I will certainly try to cope. But that gnawing pain and emptiness is my new normal. So I am not crazy after all.

As a single-parent family it always felt to me like it was my three children and me against the world. As a result, we were very close. We had our differences, yet encouraged each other's individualism. We faced many challenges in life but always got through it together. Together. That was the key to our family. Losing Monique in such a violent, senseless manner was just unfathomable to her siblings and me. We had no previous experience with death within our small intimate family, and it would not have helped us in this situation anyway.

My mother died of cancer when I was eleven years old. She thought she was doing the right thing in telling her children to be strong at her funeral by not wearing black and not crying. However, she did not understand the cycle of grieving. We can try to control it—this thing called grief—and put it in a box, but it will rear its ugly head at some point and time in our life.

By obeying my mother's orders, it took me a good fifteen years just to be able to start dealing with her death. Denying she even existed seemed to lessen the pain. I intentionally removed her from my consciousness because the pain was too great. This strategy seemed to work for a while; I could not remember what she looked like, smelled like, sounded like or even her touch, and that put my grief over my mother's death on hold. But when my grief over the loss of my daughter had to be dealt with as grown woman and a mother myself, the floodgates could not be shut. I was overwhelmed by my sorrow. My feelings of despair were palpable.

Then add in the cultural elements—the presumption of the need to act strong—and you have a woman who does not know how to handle grief. At Monique's funeral, a good intentioned pastor told me not to cry because others would be upset. Good luck with that one. In the Black community, particularly in the Baptist church, all those woes were given to God. But when it is God whom you feel let you down, where do you go? I had no clue as to where to go. All I knew was that I could find no solace in the institution of God. So I left the Baptist church.

Hatred and anger became my new companions. I felt betrayed—deeply betrayed—by both God and the community to which I had given and sacrificed so much. I couldn't understand why God had let this happen to me. I had been raised in the Church; I was the daughter of a minister and our church's musical director. My life revolved around service to God and service to God's children. And I had raised my own children the same way. Why then, would He allow one of them to be taken away from me?

And the horrifying irony that one of my own students, Tyrone Wells, was the catalyst in the cascading series of events leading to that ultimate and deadly December conflagration was more that I could bear. I had devoted everything I had—intellectually, physically, and emotionally—to the children of the Parkway Community. I believed in my soul that education was their ticket out of a life of poverty, crime, and violence. I gave up time with my own family, I jeopardized my health, poured my heart and soul into serving that community so that their children could have a chance at a better life. But the thought that members of that community that I had sacrificed so much for would deny my own child her life and deny her child a life with his mother—I just couldn't accept it. I couldn't fathom it. All I knew was the anger and the hatred that was building and festering within me.

With the murder of Monique, my surviving children and I suddenly found ourselves in a position in which we could not help each other emotionally the way we always had. Both Richard and Tamora suffered at their baby sister's funeral, but remained strong for the public as was expected of them. Oh how that false face caused us great difficulties in private.

Each one of us handled our grief differently. Instead of coming together and sharing our pain, we stayed apart. The reality of Monique not being alive and present at family functions and in day-to-day life became the epitome of suffering for us. I found I could not look at or be around my surviving children very much, because all I would see was the absence of Monique. I could not be around their children very much, because they reminded me that Monique was not there. We avoided talking about Monique, because her absence hurt so much. But that "elephant" was always in the room—our missing *Joy*.

As a family we went through phases and processes to try to remain "normal" and to act like we were handling our tragedy in an admirable manner. Outsiders were always commenting on how well we adjusted to our fate. It was all an act, however. All a show. We each stayed busy trying to adjust and to keep on living. Richard, stoically, took the lead in handling many of the details right after his sister's death: picking up her car, dealing with the funeral arrangements, organizing for the disposal of her apartment and her furniture and belongings, dealing with the police and the press. He used to be a bit of a Casanova, but after Monique's death he became more serious, more focused on what he wanted out of life.

When Tamora and I spoke, she never seemed to exhibit signs of her stress or sorrow. But I knew my baby was suffering. In her victim impact statement, at the conclusion of the trial and prior to sentencing, Tamora graphically explained her reaction to the news of her baby sister's death:

"I fell directly on the ground and started screaming. Where is my little sis? This couldn't be happening! I rushed to the airport to catch the next flight out to Sacramento. I'm crying so hard that I can't breathe. The woman at the ticket counter kept asking if I was okay and everyone gathered around me pestering me with all these questions. I looked at the television and there's a picture of my sister's body covered on the ground next to her SUV and my nephew, Jayden, in the arms of a firefighter. It hit me that this is real. My sister had all these dreams of a better life for her and her son and one careless reckless event that didn't even involve her took her life away."

After burying her baby sister, Tamora was placed under 72-hour observation at a mental health facility to deal with her grief. That is the level of devastation that a single bullet can produce. Even though my children were very close, Tamora couldn't bring herself to come to her brother or to me for help. I wanted to make it all better for her, but I found myself asking her over and over again if she ever thought about Monique. And each time, Tamora would get angry with me. Finally, one day she reminded me that people grieve differently, but that it doesn't mean that they loved Monique any less. It took me some time to process that fact.

At times I was resentful that my children had, in my perception, moved on and, I imagined, forgotten about their sister. But I was ever so wrong. Their friends would tell me of occasions where they had to comfort and encourage them in their times of distress. But those two would never show this side to me. At times I felt quite inadequate at my inability to support my children during this grieving process because I was mentally ill with sorrow. From my perspective, I feel part of the reason they wanted to disassociate themselves from me was that they remembered Mama being a pillar of strength. It bothered them that I had begun to make poor choices in dealing with my grief: displaced anger erupting at odd times, excessive gambling, and self-medicating with brandy, wine, and Grand Marnier. After losing the custody battle over Jayden, I began to wonder if I even wanted to live. Perhaps it would be better to join my daughter in the afterlife, I mused.

The thought of me being weak, lost, and even at times suicidal was too frightening for my surviving children to handle. They truly feared that they were not just losing Monique, but that I would soon follow. When they did speak to me, it would be in a very harsh tone, trying to shock me back into reality.

The negative effects of street violence were having a rippling effect on those who loved and cherished Monique. That violence had engulfed my family; and the Black Hole of grief was pulling us in.

CHAPTER 15

Change Is Not Part of My Persona

THE FIRST TIME I LAID eyes on the man who murdered my daughter felt completely surreal. We were in a small courtroom where the six defendants would begin the legal process for the roles they played in Monique's death as well as for injuries suffered by four additional bystanders. It was in May, 2011. Just four short months earlier our lives had been shattered, our family destroyed, I'd buried my youngest daughter, and lost custody of my grandson; and all these horrific events were due to the six defendants that were being charged this day for Monique's murder.

Perhaps not surprisingly, I had been too traumatized throughout the previous months to give much thought to these gangsters that now sat before me. But this day, prior to the beginning of the proceedings, I felt myself disengage from my body. I looked down on the people and the activities happening in the courtroom as if from above. This out-of-body experience, this dreamlike state, was a defense mechanism: detaching my mind, body, and soul from such a painful situation was the only way I could possibly cope. My mental escape was short-lived, however. As the officers brought the prisoners in, dressed in an orange jail suits, with shackles on their wrists, around their waists, and on their ankles, and placed them—one at a time—in a holding pen with heavy metal bars, I was brought joltingly back to reality.

The holding pen, I assume, was for the protection of the courtroom and possibly for the defendants themselves. The judge and various lawyers would speak to the defendants and each would respond from this restricted area. During these arraignment proceedings, charges were read against Matthew

McKinney, Michael McKinney, Ronnie Smith, Cody Wells, Jr., Cameron Taylor and Demetrius Tanner. The latter two, Taylor and Tanner, pleaded guilty to voluntary manslaughter and were each given twenty-one-year prison sentences. It would be another three years before I would see the other four finally brought to trial.

But on that spring day, I looked closely at each of these young men and tried to analyze their personalities. Due to the level of carnage they had inflicted at the crime scene, surely they must look like horrific, mutated, demonic monsters. Anyone who could kill my innocent daughter and make her son a motherless child could not possibly be human. To my astonishment each and every one of them looked like a student I had taught, or a neighbor's son, or even an extended family member.

Questions began running through my head. How did they become so twisted? Do they understand the ramifications of their actions? How would they feel if that stray bullet had killed their child? Do they have hearts, feel any remorse? Do they experience sleepless nights like mine? How did men of this caliber enter our world? Will justice be served?

Six men were charged with Monique's murder, but I really only wanted *one* to suffer. The one who recklessly and irresponsibly fired the deadly .38 caliber bullet that pierced Monique's heart. Police had already determined that the gun had been fired by Ronnie Smith. I wanted this particular gangster to experience the all-consuming pain that our family felt on a daily basis.

As the man who killed my daughter was placed in his cage, my eyes examined every inch of him from head to toe. I wanted his physical description etched into my mind to give a face, a name to the man who had ruined our lives. He was approximately five-foot-seven, of dark complexion, wore dreadlocks and an orange colored jump suit, and was shackled like the others. I tried my hardest to "mean mug" him; but he never said a word and never raised his eyes from the floor. Not only had he cheated me out of watching my daughter raise her beautiful child but now, he was cheating me from being able to display all the hatred and anger I had through my eyes.

Then my thoughts drifted back to the blessed day Monique was born—January 17, 1980. Just about a year prior to that date, I learned, her killer was born. Monique was a responsible law abiding citizen trying to raise her child in peace. The other was a gangbanger, a menace to society wreaking devastation and destruction in the lives of many. What karma, what fate, what God, what Devil had arranged for these two polar opposites to cross each other's paths? Once again, I was trying to make sense out of a senseless situation.

It took less than ten minutes for Monique's murderer to be charged and briskly escorted back to jail. Just ten short minutes and he was gone for the moment. Ten terrifying minutes through a hailstorm of bullets and Monique was gone forever.

The stress of the arraignment proceedings coupled with saying goodbye to my grandbaby Jayden was almost unbearable. At first, I experienced the sweats thinking about Jayden living in a new environment. All this kid had known since the day of his birth was his mother and the Nelson family. Would Jayden's father and new family fully accept him? Would Kenyatta's girlfriend resent Jayden's presence, knowing he was the product of a previous relationship? Would his newly fused family remain together under this level of stress? I was going crazy with worry.

I admit I am a person who is always over the top. I am always trying to find the lesson or purpose in any situation. I believed that Monique wanted me to take care of her baby. He was the greatest love of her life, and she had stipulated as much in her last written statement. With the justice system ignoring Monique's wishes and awarding the custody of her little boy to Kenyatta, I was still determined to stay in Jayden's life one way or the other. When I lost custody of Jayden and his father relocated him to Southern California, I went against all odds and all behaviors characteristic to me.

A person such as myself likes stability and bristles at change. I had lived in Sacramento since 1970. I had married and divorced there, raised my children there, and bought a house which I planned to retire in. I had completed my education and worked hard to rise through the ranks of public education to become an administrator of more than one of Sacramento's public schools. I'd been an active participant in Sacramento's community theatre. I had family, friends, colleagues—a wide circle of community and support in Sacramento. All my doctors and therapists were there! Forty years of building that community, that circle of support.

Change is not part of my persona. I am a Capricorn—a person who embraces stability. I'd even had the same telephone number for thirty years. But when Jayden was forced to move to Southern California that spring after his mother's tragic death, without a second thought I sold my house and left my life in Sacramento behind. Desperate to follow my grandson I, too, relocated to Southern California where I could more easily exercise my visitation rights and be a stable fixture in his life. I found a comfortable two-bedroom apartment in the quaint community of Toluca Lake that was just six blocks from my daughter, Tamora.

Secretly, the move was also my saving grace because the memories of Monique's tragedy and the life I had known in Sacramento haunted me in that city. I needed to take flight if I was to survive Monique's death. I am not fond of living in an apartment but the price of real estate in Southern California is far beyond my means. In retrospect, it was a gutsy move on my part, because I knew no one but Tamora and had no plan for the future. Love is blind, I guess. I never focused on what I wanted or even dealt with my fear of change at my age. All I could focus on was my need to be near Jayden. Monique had requested us to love Jayden as our own son in her will and I did.

Richard, good son that he is, handled most of the logistics in moving me to the Los Angeles area and seemed to accept and support my motive. He seemed to understand that I could no longer live in Sacramento. That with Monique's life and death haunting me on a daily basis and my role as a grandmother to this particular child looming over me, I had to move. In retrospect, however, I see that in my overzealous attempts to do right by Jayden, I overlooked how Richard may have actually perceived my giving all to Monique's child and less to his family. He never expressed any resentment, but looking back I wonder how this could not have been so? Over time, as Jayden has adapted to his new family and life, each year I find that I can let go more and spread my love throughout the family. But during that awful year after Monique's death, I had one single focus. And my children were forced to accept that I had lost Monique and I was trying to "fix it" in some weird way.

I wasn't sure if it would help, but I hoped my presence could possibly be a benefit for Jayden's transition. Remarkably, after just a few short months of implementing the visitation schedule, I realized that Jayden seemed to be adjusting just fine. How resilient little people can be.

As I started to exhale, however, Jayden's father delivered me another blow. I'd been living in the Los Angeles area for about six months. It was the summer of 2012. Out of the blue Kenyatta announced that his family was moving to Texas. And they were taking Jayden with them. Damn!

CHAPTER 16

The Scales of Justice Weigh Heavily On All

THE SCALES OF JUSTICE PROVED slow in balancing. Shortly after the initial arraignments, two of the men involved in the shootout—Cameron Taylor and Demetrius Tanner—pleaded guilty to voluntary manslaughter. They were each given twenty-one year sentences. However, the trial of the four remaining defendants wouldn't begin until June 23, 2014.

And when it finally came about, those four were tried in the Sacramento Superior Court system with a jury of someone else's peers. This was a criminal case involving people of color. Not one person of color served on that underrepresented jury. I am convinced that the outcome would have been considerably different with representation from jurors who understand the lives of diverse people in diverse situations. For one thing, meaningless excuses for bad behavior would not have been considered simply because of where a defendant resided, as was the case in this trial. I point this out because, at the end of the trial, one of the jurors who'd been interviewed by the press admitted their decision was based on their perception that in the neighborhoods where the defendants lived "they *had* to have guns." Excuse provided and accepted by people who have a stereotyped notion of what is necessary to survive in a predominantly Black community.

Sacramento Superior Court Judge Nicholas Haberman presided over the trial. Ronnie Smith and Cody Wells, Jr. were defended by attorneys Jack Beauchamp and William Eckland. Those two attorneys teamed up in opposition to the McKinney brothers' attorneys Mark Lowe and Felicia Anderson, a public defender. In their opening statements the four defense lawyers each blamed the other attorneys' clients for the events that led to the death of my daughter. Each attorney argued that their client should not be charged with Monique's murder because their client was acting in "self-defense" during the shoot-out.

Deputy District Attorney Sophia Crowne knew better. Monique would still be alive had the defendants not opened fire in the first place, she told the jury. "You will find beyond a reasonable doubt that every one of them is responsible, legally responsible, for the death of Monique Nelson." She further stated that if DeAndre Tanner had not himself died during the incident he, too, would be on trial for murder. As it turned out none of the men on trial were charged in DeAndre's death, because he had been party to the melee.

"In the end, what you're going to find is that Monique Nelson died protecting her child when these four people, along with DeAndre Tanner, Demetrius Tanner and Cameron Taylor brought their battle to the streets of Sacramento, in that location, and they turned that location at one o'clock in the afternoon, eleven days before Christmas, into a war zone," Crowne said in her opening statement. Her words were reported in the Sacramento Bee the next day.

Trials are supposed to be about justice. The family of the injured—or in our case the murdered—person goes into a trial seeking justice. But what no one could have prepared us for was the pain that comes with rehashing the events of that awful day. Or the pain that accompanies the gory details of the investigation or results from the unwillingness of the accused and their attorneys to accept any personal responsibility for what happened to our loved one.

A rationally minded person might contemplate what could possibly have occurred to create the perfect storm of violence that occurred at the barbershop that day? I certainly consider myself to be rational. But after hearing the details that led up to this particular shootout, it still makes no sense to me.

We were reminded that it started with the assault on Tyrone Wells, my former student, and the theft by Matthew McKinney of Wells' marijuana, his gold teeth jewelry, and forty dollars in cash. In retaliation DeAndre Tanner later accosted and beat up McKinney. On the day of the shooting, Cody Wells, Jr. and his buddy Marquis Pettigrew had gone into the barbershop prior to the arrival of the McKinneys. Wells was packing a .40-caliber pistol. The McKinneys carried an AK-47 assault rifle and a TEC-9 semi-automatic handgun. When Wells spotted the McKinney brothers, he pulled out his cell phone and called Ronnie Smith. Smith in turn contacted DeAndre Tanner. Shortly thereafter, DeAndre Tanner drove up with his cousin Demetrius Tanner and a buddy, Cameron Taylor. Tanner carried a 9 mm handgun that was determined didn't work. Smith arrived in a separate car; he was carrying a .38 special.

According to trial testimony, the McKinneys started firing from inside the barbershop, but quickly took the gunfight outside to the parking lot. The Tanner cousins along with Taylor approached from across Stockton Boulevard. DeAndre was fatally wounded somewhere between the street and the barbershop's front door. Smith, who had parked his car on the other side of Lindale Drive, fired on the McKinneys. A bullet from his gun hit Monique as she covered Jayden's body with her own to protect him from the melee.

Attorney Jack Beauchamp told the jury that Matthew McKinney entered the barbershop wearing the TEC-9 on a shoestring around his neck like some sort of a pendant, "a necklace of death, if you will," he described it. Further, while Matthew was in the chair getting his hair cut, his brother Michael "started doing a rap dance inside the barbershop, threatening to shoot the place up." According to Attorney Beauchamp that behavior made Wells nervous enough to call Smith for backup. Beauchamp described the atmosphere in the barbershop as "tranquil, it's quiet, it's festive, and it's peaceful until the McKinneys walked in. Then everything drastically changed."

Beauchamp claimed that Wells felt trapped in the back of the barbershop by the McKinneys. He fired twice in an effort to make his way out. The lawyer insisted his client had nothing to do with the on-going feud between DeAndre Tanner and the McKinney brothers, claiming "This was not his fight."

Felicia Anderson and Mark Lowe, attorneys for the McKinney brothers didn't deny that their clients brought the AK-47 and the TEC-9 into the barbershop, but their argument was that it was not clear who had control of which weapon. Anderson placed the blame on Wells saying he called Smith "not because he's trapped, not because he feels uncomfortable, but because he knows the enemy is there and it's time to do something...Basically, what happened is Cody Wells, Jr. is calling the cavalry. 'Come on down, the McKinneys are trapped. Let's take care of business.'" Anderson insisted it was the McKinneys who were trapped. "Nobody else."

In a parallel version, Mark Lowe called the McKinneys "marked men" and said that was the reason they had armed themselves. "Some may say that was not the best choice, but as it turns out, it was the only choice," was his excuse on their behalf.

William Eckland, Ronnie Smith's attorney, told the jury that Smith had driven to the barbershop with the sole purpose of helping his friends. Eckland painted the McKinney brothers as the ones who came running out of the barbershop firing wildly in every direction, Matthew still wearing his barber's cape, blasting the TEC-9 and killing DeAndre Tanner. "Mr. Smith fired back [from across the street] in an effort to defend himself and others who had been fired on by the McKinneys," Smith's attorney stated.

And it went on and on. We had to endure months of this storytelling and positioning between defendants related to the demise of my daughter.

During my tenure in the Sacramento City School District, I was involved in a number of tragedies experienced by families in our school communities. Tragedies such as domestic violence, shootings, suicide, hit and run car accidents, illnesses and the like usually affecting an innocent young student. I tried to support the families to the best of my ability by being empathetic, raising financial support, making home visits, attending heart-breaking funerals, quoting scriptures, listening to their individual stories and, in hindsight, giving what I now know was ridiculous advice. My prayer was that, in some way, my involvement would help to ease their tremendous pain during their time of need.

Not until the tragedy was *my* child, my nightmare did I really get it. Not until I walked in the shoes that those parents had to walk did the tragedy become real to me. I had no idea of the pain these people were experiencing. I had no idea until December 14, 2010 and again at that trial in June of 2014, how deep the Black Hole of grief can be. To lose a child, a loved one that I carried nine long months in my belly, that I nurtured and raised for eighteen years, with whom I experienced the highs and lows of life even into adulthood—not until I lost that lifeline could I truly understand the meaning of long suffering.

It still boggles my mind how much pain the human spirit can endure and still be considered alive. I would like to go back in time and apologize to the people I thought I was helping to let them know when I arrogantly said, "I understand what you are going through," that I was unknowingly telling a lie. Today I get it. It's unimaginable. Realistically, there is nothing I could have said to ease their pain. Just like there is nothing that can be said to me to mend my broken heart. All I could have done was to be present for those traumatized families.

The trial went on for over four months. And my pain was only to get worse.

CHAPTER 17

A Convoluted Animal

Twenty-plus airline flights back and forth to a city that I had come to despise. Sitting day after day in that courtroom. Feeling hopeless and helpless in a judicial system that had too many wild cards, especially where the jury and those four theatrical defense attorneys were concerned.

Watching these young men and listening to their attorneys twist the facts to try to escape culpability, seeing enlarged versions of the crime scene photos, being confronted with the autopsy photos and the actual weapons that were involved in the carnage—all were like daggers to my heart on a daily basis. As was listening to the way they talked about Monique.

Even the barber, who had established a relationship with Monique and who had been so patient with Jayden calling him "Little Man" when he was sitting in his chair, took on an entirely different attitude during the trial. To my shock he became a vulgar and hostile witness. His verbal communication, body language, lack of respect, disregard for my daughter's murder and defiant behavior was just beyond despicable. And added salt to my wound.

The most offensive experience in my daughter's murder trial happened during the closing arguments for Ronnie Smith, the man whose bullet actually killed my daughter. His defense attorney, William Eckland, in an effort to mitigate his client's involvement, began by demeaning the significance of my daughter's murder. He had the audacity to say that if Monique had been of Middle Eastern descent, a terrorist, or even Bin Laden and had been killed by a stray bullet, the level of emotionalism and media coverage in this case would never had happened. He further stated that it was a good thing that Monique did what she did (shield her baby) because the child lived. Then he continued by citing a case from the news where a woman was inadvertently shot by the police in a hostage situation. "They didn't prosecute the police for killing this woman," he sneered.

How insensitive and despicable can these lawyers be toward the victim's family and the victim's memory? That man's disrespect toward a young mother who had made the ultimate sacrifice because of the actions of his client was and is unconscionable.

The entire process, from the preliminary arraignment hearings through the subsequent murder trial, took four years to complete. The emotional highs and lows in trying to obtain justice for Monique were ambiguously complicated. That experience provided me with more information about the judicial system than I could ever want or need in a lifetime. The shenanigans that lawyers play, the policies and procedures that hinder judges from doing the right thing, and the lack of experience and knowledge of the juries all scream for organizational reform. Justice is just a concept to dream about with all the politics and extenuating factors that impede progress.

In all fairness, there are individuals within the judicial system who are dedicated and committed to making a difference in the lives of all involved. Yet on the flip side, the courtroom can be more about theatrics—who perfects the best performance to influence the minds of jurors who have no knowledge of the law, where facts can be manipulated to make subjective and convoluted decisions. It seemed, in our case, that rarely was the victim's perspective or best interest taken under consideration, but that the criminals' points of view and excuses for bad behavior were always the focal points.

It is also amazing how much information is kept from the victim's family in a murder investigation. It was only in the courtroom that I learned to what degree my daughter suffered after that fatal shot. I was always under the impression and had been informed that Monique had died instantly from her wound. This understanding provided me with some solace that my daughter's last moments were not painful. But the reality proved different. The District Attorney arranged a meeting prior to the pathologist taking the stand so we could see the pictures that would be displayed from Monique's autopsy. We were told that they did not want any emotional outbreaks in the courtroom.

The picture we were shown displayed my youngest child sprawled face down on the ground with her arms stretched over her head. Monique's sweater was pulled up to reveal a huge bullet hole in her torso. The District Attorney and the Victim's Advocate were very supportive and empathetic to our family during this process. My greatest fear was that I would lose control and embarrass my family and myself in front of the jury, the judge and the public. The pain was clearly evident on everyone's face but we managed to handle this horrific meeting also.

The next day in court, the pathologist methodically went through his findings from Monique's autopsy. The most startling new evidence was how she died. The .38 caliber bullet had entered her back torso, severed her spleen, traveled through both lungs and lodged into her heart. This was the first time I had heard this fact. It took my baby ten to fifteen minutes to die, I learned that day. That means she felt unspeakable pain, experienced difficulty in breathing, and realized death was imminent, all while lying in her two year old son's arms for the last time.

As a parent, I'd always felt it was my responsibility to keep my child safe from harm. But if my child had to die, my only hope was that she did not suffer. After hearing the pathologist's testimony, I was devastated.

Trying to get justice in the court system for Monique was an arduous, surreal, frightening, painful, and an exacerbating experience; but it gave me a razor-like focus and purpose, which I desperately needed after Jayden moved to Texas.

At the very first press conference held at the crime scene back in December of 2010, community leaders had urged citizens to come forward with the information needed to catch the gang members and to take the community back from gang violence. However when these community leader's presence was really needed while fighting for Monique's justice in the Sacramento

Superior Court system, these outraged individuals were nowhere to be found. Sometimes it seems like support only goes as far as a person's political agenda within eye's view of a news camera. Apathy hurts. Apathy kills.

I was determined not to let apathy win. I knew it was imperative to involve as many supporters in the process as I could to let the courtroom know that Monique was not just another forgotten Black statistic. She was divinely loved, a mother, and an integral part of our family and the community.

I turned to social media to contact all those who knew her and had expressed an interest in getting justice for Monique during the process. Using email, I messaged a number of supporters regularly with updates and invitations to the court sessions to humanize the victim, Monique. So often the victim is lost in the so-called process of justice because the criminals are singing so many sorry songs that they get more attention. I had Buddhists chanting, Christians praying, and well-wishers voicing their concern and support for Monique. And on many occasions, my efforts were well rewarded with supporters showing up to court sessions, wearing "Justice for Monique" t-shirts and sending "demand for justice" messages into the universe. Lip service is one thing, but those who truly loved Monique were present, vocal and visible.

This effort to mobilize on Monique's behalf did not heal the wound of grieving, however, nor did it even promote a scar. But in fact it became a diversion to the healing process. Why? Because I had to relive the events of December 14th, 2010 over and over again. An analogy of a fish that is caught on a hook comes to mind. The captured, disempowered fish who was minding its own business is pulled into an environment totally unfamiliar and contrary to its very existence. The poor fish keeps flopping, fighting, and gasping to breathe, but to no avail. Against its will and in opposition to its physical, emotional, and spiritual condition it is forced into a situation in which it is totally powerless and ultimately dies. That's how I felt during the time of the legal process. I came near to dying, both emotionally and physically.

Initially, we had a District Attorney who was committed to putting the bad guys behind bars and had a track record to accompany it. However, the powers-that-be changed District Attorneys after the two-year preliminary hearing. The new Deputy District Attorney, Sophia Crowne, had our support and confidence, and she seemed more than capable of handling a case of this magnitude. But in the end, our family considered the final verdicts to be a huge loss. On stronger days, I entertained the fact that everything happens for a reason. Plus my growing obsession with watching murder cases on the news and on television revealed numerous cases where justice was not at all served in the courtroom. We're dealing here with imperfect people in an imperfect world.

When it came time for the verdict, that jury of someone else's peers acquitted Cody Wells, Jr.—the man whose phone calls brought the Tanners and Smith to the barbershop to kill the McKinney brothers—of all charges. They allowed that young man to walk freely out of the courtroom even though the evidence proved beyond a shadow of a doubt that he was intimately involved in the crime. If this young gangbanger had not made those fateful phone calls that day, my precious Monique would still be alive today.

Apparently the jury bought attorney William Eckland argument that Monique's death was over-sensationalized and that Ronnie Smith's bullet was inadvertent when it hit her. Instead of an outcry of disdain for this lethal person, this jury of someone else's peers downgraded his client's charges. Ronnie Smith was only found guilty of voluntary manslaughter and use of a firearm, not of first-degree murder. At his sentencing, he was given only twenty-one years, much less than he would have received had he been convicted of murder. Once again, negative behavior gets rewarded.

I was livid about this verdict, because the law states that if criminals are engaged in mutual combat, mutual consequences should follow. This jury bought the attorneys' spin that Smith, even those he clearly chose to drive to the barbershop fully armed and knew that a fight was imminent, shot back in self-defense.

Of the entire group, only Matthew McKinney and Michael McKinney were found guilty of first-degree murder. To show their callous lack of respect for the court, Matthew and Michael McKinney taunted the jury upon hearing the verdict by tearing off their dress shirts right in front of everybody, thus exposing the tattoos running up and down their arms and necks that had been concealed during the trial.

The sentencing hearing for the McKinney brothers was its own nightmare. The two convicted men decided to again flaunt their callous disregard for the court. By law, these brothers were required to listen to the family's victim impact statements and to watch a short photo video of their victim. The prior defendants had shown some modicum of respect during their sentencing and even apologized for killing my precious daughter. But not the McKinney brothers. They made a point of looking annoyed and could be heard loudly muttering and complaining to their attorneys. They unleashed profanities and refused to look at the video of Monique, remaining unscrupulously rebellious to the end.

Reporter Stanley Chan posted this on the Sacramento Bee's website afterward: "At their sentencing on Friday, the two [McKinney brothers] revealed a little more about themselves – loudly muttering to each other and their lawyers while the mother of the young woman killed in the Dec. 14, 2010, barbershop shootout delivered her victim impact statement..." (www.sacbee.com; October 24, 2014).

The sentencing hearing was meant to be opportunity for the defendants to seek leniency by displaying any slight hint of remorse for their actions in front of the man who had their future in his hands—Nicholas Haberman. Instead the McKinneys' behavior and comments were so despicable that the judge had to intervene. When it was my turn to speak, I bluntly asked the two men if they understood the long-term consequences of their actions and what they had done to my daughter, to her child, to me, and to my family.

Neither man answered, so Judge Nicholas Haberman repeated my question, "Do you understand the long-term consequences of your actions?" Getting no response, he answered his own question stating that the answer was clearly "No!"

When the judge asked if they had anything to say, Michael McKinney finally blurted out, "Yes, sir. She don't know what this is doing to *my* mom. She don't know what I was going through when I was out there and they were shooting at me."

Moments later, when the judge was making his own final comments, Michael rudely cut him off, speaking again about me. "She don't know what I went through. She don't know the reason why I carried the gun, people shooting at my car while I'm driving my car." He went on to make excuses about his life and lack of resources and to complain that he had become a target.

Judge Nicholas Haberman wasn't interested in excuses. He reminded the young man that, regardless of the circumstances, he had chosen a dangerous lifestyle

"Yep, I chose it, and you're going to give me what you're going to give me," was the comeback. The judge gave him fifty-three years and four months to life in prison. His brother Matthew earned fifty-two years and eight months to life. The judge added time for the shootings of the other four innocent bystanders, all of whom survived, but the bulk of the time to be served was for Monique's murder.

The concept of justice is a convoluted animal. We seek justice for our deceased loved ones but in the end is justice really served? Is there fair play when the victim is in a mausoleum and the criminals get away with a jail sentence? Can I visit my loved one in a jail cell? Can I hold and kiss her again? Will my grandson ever have the opportunity of knowing and loving his mother? My family did not feel vindicated at the sentencing nor was there a sense of closure for this chapter of our lives. All we experienced was an agonizing emptiness. The emptiness of knowing we will never see my daughter again. She went to get her family Christmas portrait taken on December 14, 2010, and that was our last portrait of her.

So much pain for so many people. When I was principal of Parkway, we focused on providing a quality, culturally relevant, instructional program, positive role models from every walk of life, and a reinforced sense of community. We institutionalized the "full service approach" to meet the needs of our students and their families, most of whom lived in and among this community of violence. One of our mantras was saying no to drugs and gangs, knowing that that life style can lead to an early grave. We further reiterated that if they needed to belong to something, needed to feel loved, feel accepted, and gain the skills and knowledge base that can lead to a bright future, we were embracing them to join our school family. We were there to support them.

I tried hard during those years at Parkway to support Tyrone Wells, the young man who inadvertently tipped the first domino in a disastrous chain of events. In a sadly ironic turn, Tyrone—who had not been party to the shoot-out but who had testified at the trial as a prime witness—was found dead just days after the verdicts were rendered. At first there was suspicion that he was murdered for defying the gang member code of not snitching. However, it was eventually revealed that his death was the result of yet another drug deal gone awry. He was shot while driving his vehicle to an unknown destination to purchase drugs. Once again, a violent shooting had terminated a life that I knew.

During the court proceedings, Tyrone had been instructed not to interact with me. He never was one to follow the rules. Outside the courtroom he ran to me and hugged me and kissed me each day before his testimony. This grown young man resorted back to the fourth-grade sweet boy I knew. He even introduced me to his fiancée with whom he had three small children. Now, due to another senseless act of violence, three more children will have to go through life without ever knowing their father. Without knowing the love and dreams he had for them.

How could I possibly bear the pain of so much violence anymore?

CHAPTER 18

The Bottomless Pit

AFTER THE TRIAL ENDED, I quickly plunged into a dark, bottomless pit of depression. Jayden's move to Texas had already nudged my fragile psyche further into the downward spiral of grief as my life spun further and further out of my control. The less than satisfying outcome of the verdicts and sentencing, combined with a sudden loss of purpose, became too much to deal with. My tear-stained face, bulging eyes, and hoarse voice were tale tell signs of a woman losing her freaking mind. Although I had two other children and one other grandson besides Jayden, my focus was on the loved ones that I had lost. Optimism was replaced with pessimism. Joy became long suffering. And thoughts of suicide clouded my mind daily.

When my daughter was murdered, I lost all of my spiritual and religious connections. I lost touch with the God I had worshipped all my life. I felt abandoned. And I could no longer see my way to forgiveness, reconciliation, or even living.

In addition to finding Monique's last will and testament in her SUV, another mysterious item of hers was given to me after the trial: a cassette from the player in her car. That cassette contained one of her favorite gospel songs, Kurt Carr's "God Blocked It."

The lyrics to this song describe the dangers awaiting the singer, the destruction that was "sure to be." In the song, Carr thanks God for angels that he perceives as shielding and protecting him, looking out for him. He declares that the devil had a plan to kill him, but then God intercepts that plan and tells the devil, "No." The theme of the song is the same as the title, insisting that "God blocked it." That God wouldn't let the singer die because He knew he "had work to do."

But my baby had work to do, too. Why didn't God intercept the devil's plan on December 14, 2010? Maybe there is more to Monique's sacrifice than my carnal eye can see. Yes, God "blocked it" for my wonderful grandson, Jayden. But He blocked it with my daughter. She was and continues to be Jayden's angel; but where was her angel?

My mother would have fainted at this admission, but the truth is at that moment I hated God. I hated Christianity and all its teachings of a loving God, Our Protector, a Just God, *just believe and love thy neighbor and good things will happen to you*—because in my life it no longer rang true. Christians are supposed to be engulfed in the protective presence of God. Where was Monique's protection? *Spirit supplies my every good*. What good can come from a thirty-year-old Christian woman being shot down in the streets of Sacramento leaving a motherless child?

This tragedy engulfed me with such a circle of devastation that I couldn't even listen to gospel music. I was raised on gospel music. I sang gospel music in numerous choirs, groups and even solo performances. But to hear it, even today, breaks my heart. Our family followed all of the golden rules, but still what I cherish most, my family as I knew it, was destroyed. What kind of God would allow such a thing to happen to an innocent mother? *If You have to spread some wrath, why not take me?* I was more than ready to go.

I could feel my surviving family fall apart, disintegrating before my eyes, but I was helpless to do anything about it. As I mentioned earlier, I couldn't stand to be around my surviving children and their families for any length of time, because the sight of them reminded me too painfully of Monique. We didn't talk very much about Monique, because it hurt so much. How could the world just go on? How could everyone just forget about my beloved Monique? I didn't realize the depth of some family members' and friends' grief, and I didn't understand that people grieve in different ways.

My relationships with my siblings, Ellouise and Beatrice, were like walking on eggshells. They desperately wanted to support me. But I could not be supported because I did not know what I needed. They couldn't give me

Monique back so what was the point, I wondered? They wanted so badly for me to pick myself up and dust myself off, be positive, be God-fearing, and proceed on with my life. Inwardly, I was angry with them for not understanding what I was going through. How could they? They had never had a child murdered. I felt like they just wanted me to accept and move on with God; but that's not me. I felt that the God we had been inundated with since birth was a mere myth, like the Easter Bunny or Santa Claus. If He were real, I reasoned, he would never have allowed Monique to be murdered. I would even find myself experiencing jealousy when they talked about their children, their grandchildren, and their families, feeling irrationally that they were bragging about their good fortunes when my family had been demolished by one damn stray bullet.

My experiences with my friends were equally challenging. I was not the same happy go lucky, fun-filled person I had been. A grieving mother can make people feel uncomfortable, so it's not uncommon for acquaintances and even friends to avoid them. Not out of like or dislike for the person—I think it is more for self-preservation. Because we are never taught properly to talk about loss, it becomes a taboo subject and makes people feel uncomfortable. Avoidance comes about because one cannot or will not deal with a situation. Trust me, some days I wished to avoid myself! Embracing avoidance may make the immediate situation easier to deal with for the sympathizer, but the lack of social contact can lead to long-term depression for the griever. It certainly did for me.

Isolation became my closest friend and my enemy. It was two-fold—emotional and physical. The physical isolation was real and was magnified by Monique's and Jayden's absence. Monique had been in the habit of visiting me frequently and I looked forward to cooking for her and playing with my grandson. Those visits comforted me with an enhanced sense of family and happiness. Once Monique was gone the loneliness moved in and stayed (it continues to this very day). The loss of her created a crater-like void that was unfillable. Unfortunately, isolation became one of my new normals during which my mind reminisced about the past and dwelt on fears of the future.

For some weird reason I felt ashamed that my daughter had lost her life. I guess it was because I was her mother; I was supposed to keep her safe.

Somehow I got the notion that it was all my fault. Interaction with others became an extremely painful experience because they had no idea of the mixed bag of emotions and self-destructive feelings that I was experiencing. Their lives, as I perceived it, were full of promise and dreams. No sun shined on my existence, so I crawled under a rock of isolation, like a leper. My depression was so severe and fostered such negativity and anger on every level that it just naturally pushed everyone away. My isolation was like a jealous lover that totally consumed me in a dark world of sadness. In this quagmire of hopelessness, all I could think of was *me*.

I tried several avenues to healthily respond to the loss of my daughter. Counseling through my HMO proved to be futile. However inadvertent, rather than being helpful it felt like the counselor was instead undermining my grief. In her attempts to advise me, she kept coming back to her own grief. "Well, how do you think I felt when I lost my brother?" she asked one time. And another time she stated, "I take antidepressants daily. They help. I'll gladly prescribe them for you." Wrong advice. I simply stopped going.

Then I tried group therapy with an organization called *Compassionate Friends*. This is a long-standing, well-regarded organization whose mission it is to provide comfort, hope, and support to any family member who has experienced the death of a child of any age. But my psyche wasn't ready for a group experience, even with an organization as highly regarded this one. During these sessions I became even more depressed and catapulted into that icky Black Hole again after listening to the heart-wrenching stories of teenage suicide, automobile accidents, and fatal diseases. Witnessing how so many people in the universe were suffering the loss of a child was not a positive problem-solving formula for me. It has proven effective for many, but it just was not for me. After these failed attempts, I decided that I was on my own in dealing with Monique's death.

One of my greatest fears all my life was not being good enough as a Christian and therefore going to Hell. I now understand that hell can be right here on earth. The poor choices I made as a result of the grieving process— isolation, displaced anger, excessive gambling, and daily self-medicating with brandy, wine and Grand Marnier—were so I wouldn't have to think. Because thinking brought pain. But those very choices, besides being self-destructive, began to create financial hardships. And so my sense of control over my life slipped further from my fingers.

During my transition into darkness, on many occasions I would watch Oprah on TV. She covered many thought-provoking topics on her shows dealing with self-help that had assisted me in the past. But with this cloud of negativity choking my mere existence, was I ready for any advice? I watched one particular episode of *Super Soul Sunday* on the Oprah Winfrey Network, in which the "pearl of wisdom" for the day for those who were suffering a loss was, "Allow yourself to feel the pain." Don't ignore it, avoid it, or deny it, viewers were advised; go ahead and experience the pain. I thought to myself, *what bullshit! Like I have a choice in not feeling the knives that penetrate my broken heart on a daily basis?* The excruciating pain of living without my effervescent Monique was the epicenter of my daily living. I could never deny the pain.

I spent a lot of time crying. They say tears of grief cleanse the soul. But my soul remained cloudy as ever. My past professional life as an administrator conditioned me to have a "Fix it!" kind of mindset. During this journey, I could not fix anything. My grandson, Jayden, was my only hope for sanity and now I had lost him too. My situation had rendered me hopeless because I could never bring Monique back.

My awareness of violence in the world became ultra-heightened as I realized how fragile life really is. I become almost obsessive as I watched murder cases on the news and on television, looking for real-life stories of other grieving mothers in my attempt to ascertain how they survived the loss of a child to gun violence.

I remained traumatized for a long, long time. Frequently, I experienced nightmarish flashbacks of seeing my once jubilant, funny as heck daughter dead in the street with a bullet lodged in her heart or lifeless and cold on that slab at the funeral parlor. These images came in and out of mind daily with no regard as to what I was doing or with whom I was speaking. I couldn't stay busy enough to prevent these images from paralyzing my entire body.

Visits to Sacramento haunted me on every level. Every damn thing reminded me of Monique and resurrected all the hurt and pain that permeated throughout my body. Time had not eased my suffering. Watching young mothers playing in the park or walking down the streets with their sons, reminded me of Monique. A mixture of feelings—anger and jealousy—consumed me on a daily basis. Why couldn't my daughter have this routine life of motherhood? What makes these women so much better or highly favored than my sweet daughter?

Hearing hip-hop or gospel music from the 80's and 90's reminded me of Monique. Watching television shows or movies that Monique and I use to watch, where familiar characters were alive and still aging reminded me that Monique was dead, Monique who had only lived a fraction of those characters' life spans. *Just not fair!*

The daily reminders that life will never be the same were overwhelming. Trust me, I know all the politically and spiritually correct advice for these issues: "Cherish the years you had with Monique." "Time heals all wounds." "Your other family members need you." "Your grandson needs you." "Find something to love and hold on for dear life." But for me and my life all they amounted to were all cliché's.

Another daily occurrence that tugged—still tugs—at my heartstrings was that California and Texas (where I visit Jayden regularly) has thousands of SUV's—taupe-colored Chevy Tahoes. And my eye always spots the ones built in the same year as Monique's vehicle. Each time I'd spot a 2008 Chevy Tahoe it reminded me—still reminds me—of that day, December 14, 2010 when a stray bullet went through the windshield and killed my *JOY*!

My ancestors were from a lineage of fighters. Their mantra was "never to give up because this too shall pass." But the hole that is created with the death of a child is always there. During those darkest of my days, I continued to lick my wounds and to cry without ceasing.

In the middle of one of my messiest meltdowns, I could not muster enough energy to get out of the bed, to clean my body, nor even to get dressed. I was married to a box of Kleenex and staring at my .38 revolver, frustrated with myself for not having the courage to pull the trigger. My screaming and wailing reached a new zenith.

And then, suddenly, the room became very still. Out of nowhere, radiating from within an incandescent golden light, I beheld my daughter, Monique. Her hair glowed a beautiful copper color, styled in a pageboy fashion. She wore a matching copper-colored cashmere sweater. Her face was exotically glamorous with her sculpted features. She wasn't smiling; but she exuded an essence of serenity.

Mesmerized by being in her presence, I held my breath and stared. Then she spoke. In a sharp, direct tone she demanded, *"Stop all that damn crying, Mama!"*

In complete shock, I did. I took a deep breath and wiped my tears. Now, if this apparition had had a sweet little angelic voice with a message of blessings and peace, then I would have known that I was dreaming. But when I heard that no-nonsense demand from Monique, I knew that was my baby. As her sister would say, *she could be a hot mess.* Monique's personality was one that demanded respect, and she was known for speaking her mind. She was speaking to me, and I was in no position to ignore her.

CHAPTER 19

Never Having Said Goodbye

SEEING MONIQUE AND HEARING HER admonition to "Stop all that damn crying!" was the kick in the pants I needed. Embracing her message, I knew it was time to regroup. Living with grief wouldn't be easy. There would be no miraculous recovery from my loss. That loss, that hole in my heart, was a forever status. But if I were to go on living, it had to be on Monique's terms. And eventually on my own terms.

No, the crying didn't stop. Not right away. And certainly not forever. But I was able to take a breath again. I was able to look ahead to the next day again. And the first thing I did, my first baby step on my path to learning to deal with my grief, was to plan how I was going to continue my regular visitations with my grandson now that he had moved to Texas. I marked my calendar for every three months—four times a year I would travel to Texas to see Jayden. Although this plan would exhaust my retirement mutual fund, "Ain't No Mountain High Enough" became my new mantra in life where Jayden was concerned.

I think one factor that made Monique's death so traumatic for me and for my surviving children was that we never got to say good-bye. One day Monique was cracking jokes in my kitchen, and the next day she was gone. No closure for those of us left behind—only regrets that we did not say "I love you" or "I'm proud of you" or a multitude of other affirmations. So, in that first year after her admonition to me, I made sure to text Richard and Tamora daily to re-affirm my love for them. Each text consisted of a quote, a "love ya" message, and a graphic of love. Thanks to the internet, Barnes and Noble, and the public library I have a wealth of quotes and messages to send from every genre, from silly to serious, and the most diverse list of authors that anyone could imagine. For example: "However long the night, the dawn will break." (~African Proverb) or "I love you for all that you are, all that you have been, and all you are yet to be." (~Unknown)

Whenever I texted my two living children, I made a point to text Monique also. I always wanted her to be included in this affirmation of love and to realize that our love transcends death. One day after sending my daily text, however, I received a mysterious telephone call that threw me for a loop. The screen of my iPhone displayed an incoming call from Monique's number. Her photo popped up on the screen, just like it always used to. Instinctively I anticipated her bubbly, cheerful voice on the other end saying, "Hey, Mom!" My breathing stopped for a moment. My mind went into shock. Had my text message reached Heaven? I cautiously answered my cell phone. "Hello?"

To my chagrin, an irritated Asian male voice demanded, "Who is this and why do you keep sending me all these text messages each day?"

I quickly apologized and explained that his phone number had belonged to someone very special to me. Mollified, he accepted my apology and hung up.

Instantly, the tears began to flow, my knees buckled, and I crumpled to the floor. I cannot adequately explain the combustion of emotions I felt in that two-minute period of time. I was terribly disappointed at not being able to talk to Monique and complete our unfinished business of saying "Good-bye". On the other hand, if she had responded I may have fainted from fright at the possibility of communicating with the other side. I had assumed that Monique's cell phone was still with the police department, stored away in a dusty box with all the other evidence from the crime. Apparently, the telephone company had already reassigned Monique's telephone number, and this poor gentleman had been receiving terms of endearment for months from a grieving mother.

If I was going to do as Monique required and stop crying 24/7 and begin to look ahead to the next day and the day after that, I needed a way to reconnect with my inner self, especially since I had given up on God. One fortuitous day, I was riding the Patty Wagon Casino Tour bus on my way to numb my despair with a bit of gambling. As I sat looking out the window waiting for the bus to roll, a woman I'd never met before slipped into the seat next to me. She told me her name was Daphne Niall. We started talking. Strangely enough, both of us were feeling a little teary-eyed that day. We had never laid eyes on each other before, but the universe seemed to have drawn us together due to a common denominator—we discovered that each of us was dealing with the loss of a beloved daughter. Her daughter had passed almost a year prior to Monique from heart failure.

Masking my feelings has never been one of my strong points, and seeing my pain this woman reached out to me. When I asked how she coped with her loss, she shared that she had been practicing Nichiren Buddhism for thirty years. One of the tenets of Nichiren Buddhism is that believers accept that a person can experience absolute happiness even during suffering. Well at this point in my life, I had put the "S" in suffering and was looking for a way out. Daphne actively encouraged me to attend a meeting at the Buddhist Center in Pasadena with her. I took her up on it.

It was through that and subsequent meetings that I learned about Soka Gakkai International (SGI) Buddhism. This form of Buddhism has its roots in the teachings of a 13th century Japanese monk named Nichiren Daishonin. Nichiren believed that the Lotus Sutra—a sort of Buddhist scripture—holds the key to transforming an individual's suffering and to enabling society to flourish. I desperately needed that kind of transformation. Whether or not following Buddhism would help me out of my despair remained to be seen. But at this point I was ready to try just about anything.

I began by learning to chant the phrase *Nam myoho renge kyo*. The nucleus of this unique practice involves chanting at least twice a day to the *Gohonzon*. The *Gohonzon* is a scroll-like object of devotion, a symbol of respect to call forth our Buddha nature from within. There are many branches of Buddhism, but SGI Nichiren's Buddhism differs because there is no high priest or priestess to honor. The Buddhist nature is believed to be within us all. No middleman needed. We chant *Nam myoho renge kyo* in quick repetitions to the *Gohonzon*, praying for ourself and for others. *Nam* means to dedicate one's life. *Myoho* is the mystic law. *Renge* speaks to the cause and effect of the mystic law and the Lotus Sutra. And *Kyo* represents Buddhist teachings.

Many of the more experienced Buddhists chant with their hands folded in front of them holding a set of beautiful beads. I never asked nor knew what the beads represented. Instead, when I chant I hold Monique's wooden beaded bracelet that I received after her murder. I pray for her happiness in the afterlife since this side was the pits. I also have a repetitious prayer request that I call the Three P's: Prosperity, Protection and Peace of Mind for myself and for others.

When I chant *Nam myoho renge kyo*, it seems to quiet the beast within me. When the nightmarish flashbacks of Monique lying dead in the street or lying lifeless on that that funeral parlor slab hit me out of the blue, previously they would paralyze me. After learning to chant, I found that the repetition of *Nam myo renge kyo*, relaxes me and allows me to get through another day. I still chant in times of need to this day. However, my complete transformation to this new spiritual practice is much like my life—a work in progress.

Through my new friend, Daphne, I found the Buddhist members to be a very loving, patient, supportive group of individuals. With their help, I turned my focus from weeping and self-pity to deepening my understanding of the Buddhist practice. A major component of this unique religious practice, I learned from them, focuses on giving gratitude for all things. My new daily routine, besides chanting, included offering the following Prayer of Gratitude for the honor and privilege of knowing and mothering Monique:

Thank you Monique for your precious life and all you have done to enrich the lives of
others. Thank you for:
The Laughter
The Camaraderie
Your Nurturing Motherhood to My Grandson
Taking Caring of Me During My Illness
Loving All of Us

Keeping Us in Check
Keeping It Real
The Wonderful Conversations
Eating All My Crazy Recipes
Being the Family Protector
Being a Respectful Loving Daughter
Being The Spoke in the Family Wheel
Giving My Life Purpose
Giving Stability
Making Me Realize That Control Is an Illusion
Being My Rock, My Sun and Stars
Looking Out For Others
Striving to Do Your Very Best
Giving Me the Greatest Grandson Ever
For Being a Beacon of Light For All to Follow
Being My Daughter and Friend
For Teaching Me How to Love
Giving the Ultimate Sacrifice to Save Your Son
Being You
I foster the highest degree of gratitude for the short thirty years that you have shared with me and others. You make your Mama proud!!!!!

Mystifyingly this Prayer of Gratitude for Monique always appears first in my Microsoft Word Program whenever I open it up. I have closed this document many times, but it always reappears as an open document in my computer program. I think Monique continues to leave her footprint throughout my life.

After Monique's death, I had become obsessed with the spiritual world in an effort to find her. I really needed to know if she was in a better place and at peace.

When I was given the opportunity to view the crime scene and autopsy photos of my daughter during the trial, I became especially distressed. I openly expressed my sufferings to Sophia Crowne, the District Attorney. At the end of the trial, she cried and shared her frustrations about the outcome with me. She reassured me that Monique was not just a statistic to her. We freely talked about my bouts of depression and the challenges of dealing with the loss of my child. I was especially upset over how long it took for Monique to pass once the bullet had lodged in her heart.

Compassionately, weeks after the trial ended Sophia sent me a card of encouragement enclosed with a book entitled, *Closer To The Light*. Researched by Dr. Melvin L. Morse and co-written by Paul Perry, this book describes the near death experiences of children and amazing revelations of what it feels like to die. The case studies in Moore's and Perry's book represent material gathered during interviews with patients who'd had a near death experience. Some of the characteristics of the near death experiences were:

- Many of the patients went through a dark tunnel into an illuminating Light.
- Some had greeters such as a friend or family members, even pets.
- The individuals experienced an overwhelming sense of Love and Acceptance.
- Some saw a figure or entity such as God.
- Some had an insatiable desire to stay on the other side but had a choice as to whether to return.
- Some had an out-of-body experience looking down on their situation.
- None of them experienced pain when they were in the Light.

Thinking of the people mentioned in the book made me think of my own Aunt Marcella, whom I loved so dearly and for whom I'd tried so hard but unsuccessfully to be there when she died. On the telephone, when my sister Ellouise told me of her death, she said that in Auntie's final minutes she appeared to go in and out of consciousness. While facing death it seemed that Auntie was aware of someone else being in the room with them.

"Indeed," my sister said, "someone had come for Auntie to take her over the threshold." According to Ellouise, Auntie rose up in her bed one time and then three additional times, reaching out to something or someone. After the fourth movement, she quietly passed over. "It was very spiritual in nature," Ellouise declared, "because Auntie was in no shape to rise up by herself one time, let alone four times. Everyone in the room witnessed it."

The author of *Closer to the Light* referred to a quote from the ancients that said: "All men must die and death is not to be feared. There is a Light that we will all experience after death, and that Light represents joy, peace, and unconditional love."

This quote brings a heightened level of peace to my life. To think that Monique may be experiencing unconditional love, joy, and peace would allow me to let her go. To think that maybe, just maybe, she is safe in the ethereal Light eases my soul. But the most enlightening of the data shared in this book was that none of the patients who'd been involved in accidents, drowning, etc. reported feeling any pain while dying. Their spirits had already left their bodies. I pray this is true. I pray that Monique suffered no pain or anguish and that she is now free, free from pain and suffering, free knowing that her baby, Jayden, is healthy, safe and happy due to her ultimate sacrifice.

But still, I had to know. I began to read books by various mediums and spiritualists, watched TV shows connected to the afterlife, and frequently visited a metaphysical and spiritual bookshop located in Sherman Oaks called Psychic Eye.

The Psychic Eye, a chain of bookshops established in 1985 by Robert Leysen and Mary Kara, bills itself as a "New and Old Age" bookstore. The establishment offers a variety of services dealing with the spiritual realm, including psychic readings at their various locations. They had a long list of psychic consultants posted on their website, along with individual bios to assist with my selection of a reader. Being new to this culture, I just closed my eyes and pointed to one. The receptionist informed me that by law psychic readings are just for entertainment and I was solely responsible for what I did with the information. I began to experience a slight anxiety attack as

I finished making arrangements for my first reading. But then I reminded myself that my own mother visited psychic readers and seemed to possess that seventh intuitive sense herself. So how bad could it be?

I was directed to a small cubby-like room with decorated curtains in place of doors. I found it to be dark and a little spooky in there with just a single lit candle on the center of the table illuminating the space. I did not have to wait long before a stunning Black woman entered dressed in gypsy-like attire with sequined scarves and jewelry to match. Oddly, she seemed a little flustered when she first entered the room, but immediately started talking to me as if she had always known me.

The psychic commented that she was still upset from her previous reading because the customer was adamant that there was no God! To my surprise, this reader believed with conviction that there is a God and that his angels were busy at work in the physical and spiritual world. Of course, I was blown away because this was only six months after my daughter's death and my belief in God was shaky too. I decided to keep my thoughts about God to myself.

We went through the typical formalities and introductions, and then she straight out asked, "Why are you here, Deborah?"

I tried to contain my emotions as I summarized the tragic events that had happened. The spiritualist listened intently. Finally I blurted out, "I'm here to try and hear from my daughter or at the very least to receive some assurance that there is a spiritual world and that Monique is alright."

To my surprise, the psychic reader said, "I remember reading about your daughter's story in the newspaper." Then she said a prayer for Monique and offered her condolences.

Being the untrusting person that I had become, I was making mental notes of everything this woman said to see if she was authentic or maybe just a charlatan regurgitating information about Monique that she had read in the newspaper.

There was no crystal ball, no tarot cards. She just held my hands as tears ran down my face, looked straight into my eyes and said, "God is real." Then she proceeded to search for Monique. Nothing more was said until finally, "I am in touch with the Spirit."

Monique's spirit? I wondered. *Whose spirit?* But I said nothing.

The Last Portrait: A Psalm For Monique

"I can see Monique's spirit leaving her physical body," she told me. "There is a male spirit there to greet her and this masculine spirit is hovering close to you."

Was it my father, Monique's grandfather? The psychic further explained that Monique was of a higher order spirit because she had sacrificed her life for another. Then she focused on my pain and grief, offered strategies germane to healing, and ended the hour-long session by telling me to "Let Monique go!" She said, "Monique is an old Spirit and she has work to do. Monique cannot complete her journey nor get through to you because of your deep grief." She explained that my grief was keeping Monique here in this world when she should be doing God's work. "If you love her, let her go!"

The familiar anger began to rise within me as I sharply replied, "That is easier said than done. You have never lost a child!"

In retrospect, I am glad that this psychic could not talk directly to Monique and that we could not hear my daughter's voice like in the movie *Ghost*. Although I desperately desired to hold and talk to my baby again, I don't think I could have handled it as an apparition. However, the psychic reader's words mesmerized me and I kept trying to use my cognitive mind to disprove what she had said. My Christian upbringing made this type of interaction taboo, so there was a niggling feeling that I was doing something wrong. But I felt no threat, no evilness or trickery from this woman. If anything, there was a moment of peace because she told me Monique was okay. That Monique was an angel of the purest form.

I went back to the Psychic Eye many times, but I could never find this particular consultant again. Experiencing readings from a variety of psychic readers, with a variety of skills, some of whom were giving common-sense advice and others who were simply great conversationalist, never quite met the expectations of the first time. Eventually, I stopped going and continued to try and find my way in a life I did not sign up for.

Grief, I have come to realize, is a natural response to loss. Psychotherapist Julie Brams-Prudeaux, on her website www.juliebrams.com, says that "grief-work is the active process of reinventing oneself in response to this loss." The thing is, that while I know the grieving will never stop, I no longer want to be defined by the violent death of my daughter.

John W. James and Russell Friedman, founders of The Grief Recovery Institute, in their book *When Children Grieve* (2002) define grief as the "conflicting group of human emotions caused by change and the end to a familiar pattern of behavior." I think the change of having your entire family destroyed by a senseless act of violence exceeds all the requirements for this definition.

Because of the change in my family's life, my search to find the true meaning and purpose for life has been a painful journey. However, there is grace and mercy in my grieving process; and that grace and mercy has always resided in my grandson, Jayden. The question for me was: Did that same grace and mercy show itself to him?

CHAPTER 20

Special Bonds

I AM NOT EXAGGERATING WHEN I say that whenever I am at my lowest ebb, whenever I can't see through the tears and the dark abyss, I will unexpectedly receive a text message or a telephone call out of the blue, from little Jayden, already eight years old at the time of this writing. Just hearing that enthusiastically loving voice is medicine for my soul. *Thank you, Monique, for such a loving child!*

Sometimes our greatest fear can prove to be our greatest blessing in life. When Jayden was taken away from me, I feared his transition to a new life with people he didn't know. However, after six long years, I have grown to love Jayden's new family, especially when I see how much they love and care for each other. Jayden's father, Kenyatta Butler, stepped up to the plate and became a "Father Extraordinaire." Thankfully, he respects and values my role as Grandmother to his son, allowing me to visit and spend time with him as often as Jayden and I like.

Shortly after Jayden moved to Texas, I went to Barnes and Nobles and bought a number of children books on loss and the grieving process, one of which used a dinosaur as the main character, because Jayden was mesmerized by dinosaurs. I sent them to Kenyatta and asked him to read them to Jayden when he felt the child was ready. I have also collected a *Library of Memories* for Jayden to

Kenyatta and Jayden

access when he is older with videos of his mother, pictures, and news articles of what happened to her—but all in his time not ours.

Kenyatta has a more direct approach; he reminds Jayden of who his biological mother was and has openly discussed Monique's death with him to let him know that his mother was a hero and about the ultimate sacrifice she made for him. The first time Jayden visited me, I showed him the oversized, framed picture in the bedroom I have set aside for him. As he gazed up at the last portrait ever taken of his mother and him, I held my breath in fear of the emotional response it might initiate. But all he said was, "Grandma, look at the white mountains behind Mama and me." Such innocence!

As he got older, more somber responses to mentions of Monique were evident; one time he even expressed anger. We were looking through an album of family pictures that included his mother, and I tenderly told him, "Your mother still loves and misses you." He responded sharply, "How do you know?"

Although Jayden seems to be a well-adjusted, happy child, it is human nature that as he grows up he will be inquisitive about who his biological mother was and about what happened to her. There is no way he can understand who he is without knowing who she was.

I was especially grateful for Kenyatta's support during the time of the trial as we strove to obtain justice for Monique in the court system. His victim impact statement detailing the effects of this tragedy on his son left many in tears and created much more awareness of how one senseless act of violence leaves an indelible mark of loss and devastation in the lives of all involved.

Dated September 2, 2014, Kenyatta's statement included these words: "Your Honor, I am writing this letter on behalf of myself and my 6-year-old son, Jayden Anthony Butler-Nelson. Your Honor, Monique Nelson is the mother of our beautiful son, Jayden. I would like to share with you how a senseless killing has affected a little boy, who if he had one wish it would be to see his mommy again. The mother who courageously paid the ultimate price for the love of our son by sacrificing her life for his. There is no greater love! My heart will always have a void knowing I will never see or speak to Monique again, but your honor it's the void that I see in our son's eyes that hurts me more than anything. It's the times that I catch him gazing out the window or just daydreaming and I ask him "what are you thinking about?" and his simple reply "my mommy." It is truly painful to see a sweet little boy who is so young be in so much pain, anguish and yearning for a mother he will never see again. For a mother who showered him with all her love and for a mother who was the center of his universe. Jayden's life is and will forever be changed. I don't know exactly what he is thinking or what he feels but I do know he misses his mommy more than any of us can imagine. It's the look of hurt, confusion and total sadness that tears me up inside. We can be in the grocery store or watching cartoons and he will just start crying for his mommy. All I can do is hold him until he settles down and tell him his mommy is watching him from heaven. I tell him he has a mother who loves him more than anything in this entire world and she is with God watching him. It hurts me deeply knowing he will live with this void in his heart for the rest of his life all because of a senseless killing..."[1]

Jayden was a toddler when the unimaginable tore his young life apart. A mother's love saved him and now love is still lifting him higher and higher. For this, I am so grateful.

The woman whom Jayden now calls "Mommy"—Keley Nicole Johnson—has been a Godsend. She and Jayden's father have provided stability, discipline, and love with their blended family. Jayden's step-mom is so special and talented that on Halloween, 2014, she shared the following poems that she had written.

<u>Their Guardian Angel</u>
(By Keley Nicole Johnson)

Mourning the loss of someone I never knew
A smile I never saw but know how warmly it shone on those who did,

---
[1] Kenyatta Butler's complete Victim Impact Statement can be found in the appendix.

An embrace I never felt but know the comfort it gave to others
A voice I never heard but I know that those who love her long to hear its song.

Mourning the loss of someone I never knew
because somewhere tonight I know her child is mourning her also
missing her smell, her face, her touch, her kiss
Too young to know she is always near for a mother's love endures forever.

Mourning in sympathy for a family I know is broken
Whose pain is too much to bear
Who sadness runs deep to their core and there is no comfort to be found
Mourning a life lost, too young, too beautiful, too soon
senselessly taken by another who will never comprehend what he has stolen
From a Mother, From a Father, From a Brother, From a Sister, From a Family,
From a Son and From the world.

Stolen what would have been, taken her future, taken her physical presence
but never her soul, it lives in the hearts that knew and loved her
and it shall never perish and it will always be near

Mourning a life I did not experience, the joy of a friendship I never knew,
feeling sorrowful to the deepest part of me, knowing it is nothing
compared to the anguish of those that have heard her laugh, held her hand,
shared a memory, seen her grow, and watched her become a mother
who gave up her very life for her son.

Although their pain will never fade, neither will their memories
Although her loved ones will go on, their lives will be forever altered
and they will all be forever changed. They will love harder and deeper,
embrace each other longer and keep each other closer for they know
how fragile life can be.

The Last Portrait: A Psalm For Monique

I did not need to know her, to know how deeply she loved,
To know God will give her soul eternal peace and rest for her
truly selfless sacrifice for the little precious boy she birthed and loved.

Mourning the empty sadness of it all for there is no reason
or understanding in this place,
only hope for better days and the joy that breaks through the pain when he smiles,
or turns his face and looks so much like her,
because of her he is here to remind them of her
and she left them all the greatest part of her to love. In eternal peace she watches them,
wishing she could ease their sorrow, because now she loves and watches from above
she is now their guardian angel.
~In Memory of Monique Nelson
Dedicated to her loving family and her son
December 19, 2010
Keley Nicole Johnson

<u>Not My Body</u>
(By Keley Nicole Johnson)

Not my body, nor my blood but my blessing
So small and so very sweet
Into my heart and soul does creep
the baby boy who came to me
and my son he came to be

Not my body, nor my blood but my soul
Never expected he would come into my life
and make my family whole

I often watch him sleeping peacefully
And I pray he dreams sweet dreams
that thoughts of sadness, pain and loss
are faraway and forgotten things

I didn't carry him for nine long months
but I carry him in my heart
I laid eyes on him and I was
in love and in awe from the very start

How he manages to laugh and smile and play
and share with me so much love and joy
after losing the one who brought him into the world
makes him my precious baby boy

I couldn't love him anymore
if by birth he was my own
because God looked down on him in his loss
and sent him to my home

When he runs to me with open arms
and says Mommy how was your day
I hug and kiss him tenderly
and hope he will always love me this way

I hope his Mother looks in on us
and is pleased with what she sees
and know that I will never fail in the responsibility given to me

That I will love her precious baby boy
and he will be my own
I will teach him to love the Lord and honor himself
and see to this until he has grown

I will raise a young man that would make her proud
So her heart would be at ease
and she will know that her son will live a life of love
and joy, just like she wanted it to be

He may not be of body
He may not be of my blood
But he was sent to me and is my blessing
This little boy I love
My heart
My soul
My joy
My love
My son
Jayden

This woman's writings take my breath away. Even under ideal situations, making a family unit work is no easy feat. But when the common ground is a sweet little boy named Jayden Butler-Nelson, immediate and extended family worked admirably together to make lemonade out of lemons. In my spiritual mind I see Monique's hand in this, making certain her only son was in a stable, loving environment.

Instead of looking at Jayden's placement in his father's home as losing a loved one, I am elated now to say I have experienced a paradigm shift. We haven't lost Jayden but we have refreshingly expanded our family base. Jayden is not alone. He has a father, a mother, a sister, a brother, and a host of external family members. Hallelujah!

CHAPTER 21

A Psalm For Monique

WHEN I LEFT DAVID LUBIN Elementary School in 2000 to work at the district office, the school's staff presented me with one of the most remarkable figurines I have ever received. It was a classic piece from the Ebony Vision Collection by the artist Thomas Blackshear called *The Comforter*. This unique figurine became a source of inspiration and defined the tenor of my subsequent work in the field of education.

The fourteen-inch sculpture of a serene, but elegant-looking Black woman with short white hair is intended by the artist to be an homage to the nurturing nature of women, a role we play throughout our lifetimes. The matronly woman in the figurine enshrouds four small children under the protection of her peach-colored cloak. An aura of peace surrounds every feature of this masterpiece of love.

The Free Dictionary online defines the verb *comfort* as "to soothe in time of affliction or distress." The noun *comfort* is defined as "a condition of well-being, contentment, and security...or a feeling of pleasurable physical ease or relief from pain or stress." Thus a *comforter* could be seen as one who comforts or soothes in times of affliction or distress, or one who brings a sense of pleasurable ease, well-being and contentment. *The Free Dictionary* even references the Christian meaning of the word *comforter* as being of "the Holy Spirit" The Holy Spirit which is the promise of the Father to all Christians.

The concept of *The Comforter* who soothes in times of affliction has many different faces for me. When the figurine was gifted to me, it was in honor of the love I tried to give, providing children in the public school system with a sense of protection and sense of family, which all acknowledged was no easy task. But then *The Comforter* came in the form of the support I received from family and friends during *my* times of crisis. Monique's role comes to mind as *The Comforter* while being my caregiver and The *Protector* exemplified by the ultimate sacrifice she made for her son. I've learned it's not uncommon for roles to change over time. At one point I am the comforter and protector. The next minute I *need* a comforter and protector. Life is cyclical. All I know right now, right at this moment in time, is that I would like to be under the arms of this woman of comfort in a safe and secure haven.

The months and early years after the death of my daughter were such a disconnected time for me. Day in and day out I resembled a member of the *Walking Dead*. No direction, no sense of purpose, no joy, no future, no hope, just a hot mess. Isolation became my companion. Family and friends would try to reach out to me in a fruitless effort to cheer me up, encourage me to take my next step. What they didn't understand was that I had no desire to take that step. Until the day Monique came to me and ordered me to stop crying. Even then, it was a long, slow process finding myself in the world again. Jayden was in a good place—as good a place as any child could be who'd so tragically lost his mother. But I couldn't seem to find my way. Even with two surviving children, a growing passel of grandchildren, and my loving, caring siblings, my psyche couldn't get past the violent death of youngest child caused by members of the very community I had sacrificed so many years for as an educator and comforter. I could no longer get a handle on my purpose in life.

Then one day my oldest sister, Ellouise, living in Davenport, Iowa pointed me in the direction of my purpose. She suggested that I find a way to memorialize and keep Monique's memory alive. This was a huge order considering my style of preference at the time was staying in denial. But after some thought, I took her advice to heart. I began to think of ways of keeping Monique's memory alive for her son, our family, and those who knew and loved her. After all, isn't this why we live? To be remembered by loved ones? I started brainstorming a number of ideas that would be appropriate.

First, I started the ongoing portfolio for my grandson, Jayden, which contained videos, pictures, journals, newspaper clippings and a plethora of information from Monique's birth to her death. The most revealing inclusion was a video clip of Monique talking and playing with Jayden. There was something about the way she would say *"Jayden"* that just touched my heart. It was with such love and pure adoration. I think for Jayden to be able to hear his mother's voice and to see her alive and well on this video will have a powerful influence on him. To hear her respond to the question, "Who has had the most influence in your life?" with the words, "My son, because he makes me want to be a better person," will lift him up in undeniable ways. These connections to his mother are priceless.

Second, I purchased two stars from the International Star Registry. There are now two stars in the heavens with their own unique names: Monique Roxanne Nelson and Jayden Anthony Nelson. Their registrations are permanently filed in the International Star Registry's vault in Switzerland. These two stars, Ursa Major RA 10h 1m 45s D 58° 19' and Ursa Major RA 10h 3m 47s D 59° 10' respectively, have a special place in the cosmos, side by side. We were assured that these stars are a permanent fixture in the sky and that it would take 200 million years for the earth to complete one galactic year to travel to a new position. At last, some stability in my life! There is something very mystical, very spiritual, about a star. It puts me in mind of an old Eskimo proverb: *Perhaps they are not stars, but rather openings in heaven where the love of our lost ones pours through and shines down upon us, to let us know they are happy.* In my mind, seeing Monique as a celestial being watching over and guiding all of us brings a certain amount of peace and warmth to my spirit. But it also is symbolic that my baby girl's spirit shines so brightly that not even a bullet can extinguish it!

Third, as part of my grief therapy, I took drawing lessons at a senior citizens' center in Burbank. I was so blessed to have Enrique Nolan, an energetic, unorthodox artist, as my instructor. I swear this man could teach a rock to draw. In one session, I was deeply depressed and teary-eyed because of Jayden's move to Texas. Usually, I had the innate ability to act my way through any situation without revealing my true feelings. However, this evening I was so shattered that I was compelled to share my story with someone. After class I cornered Enrique and told him the entire tragic story. I shared how I had failed my daughter by not being able to stay closely connected in Jayden's life.

The Last Portrait: A Psalm For Monique

Enrique was not an extremely emotional sort, but he listened intently and respectfully to my dilemma. Then I asked him if he would do me a favor. I wanted to hire him to immortalize my daughter by painting a portrait of her for me. In addition, I shared with him about the visitation I'd had from Monique after her death and how radiant and serene she appeared to be. To my total delight, Enrique agreed to paint his interpretation of my daughter free of charge. I gave him a picture of Monique and Jayden and left him alone for several months to work his magic.

The painting he produced was just unbelievable! When he delivered the finished product, I stared at it for hours and hours. Enrique had mastered all of Monique's physical features, especially her hands. She was portrayed as an angel lovingly smiling and looking down on her only son, Jayden, with a globe-like image of the world behind him. Enrique's painting encouraged me to have no fear; whether Jayden lived in Texas or anywhere in this world, Monique would be near to guide and protect him.

Lastly, I had been visiting Monique's mausoleum whenever I was in Sacramento. On the first Mother's Day after her death family members, friends, and I congregated there, lit candles, and expressed our undying love for my baby. Jayden had signed a Mother's Day card and I place it in front of her tomb with color-coordinated flowers. However, I always found it difficult to visit Monique's final resting place, because that is not how I wanted to remember my effervescent daughter. Therefore, I needed another setting in Sacramento to memorialize her.

Thoughts flooded my mind on how in happier times Monique and I would visit McKinley Park and push Jayden around the duck pond and rose garden in his stroller. I can visualize her looks, her movements, and the conversations that we had on these outings. I called to inquire how to install a memorial bench in the park in her honor. I was informed that this was not a possibility but that I could purchase a spot in the Rose Garden in memory of Monique. I made a special visit to the park and found the most beautiful pink rose bush located near a bench facing the sun. This was the spot that I wanted to visit to cherish the good times that I'd had with my daughter and grandson at her favorite park. I purchased a plaque inscribed with "In Memory of Monique Nelson." Visitors and family members could sit on the bench, read a good book, rest in the sun, and smell the alluring fragrance of roses while honoring my youngest child. This memorial was much more fitting and psyche-friendly to me than the traumatic visits to the cemetery.

Keeping Monique's memory alive has become my life's mission. My big sister was right! It has given me a positive focus and a purpose. My greatest dream would be for this book that I have written in honor of Monique to be a catalyst for some other mother, father, or family member to change their lifestyle immediately. My message to them: *Cherish and embrace your loved ones right now.* Make them a priority above your job, money, and all the superficial things that we worship in our lives. The infantile arguments we hold onto just to be on top, just to make a narrow point—let them go! Any wrongs that need to be righted, forgive them; forgive yourself and just let them go! Because in the big picture of life, all those distractions to love just don't matter.

In a mega-second, we can lose our loved ones; we can lose it all! I know only too well.

CHAPTER 22

Many Paths

MANY TIMES I HAVE THOUGHT about and drawn an analogy between my life's tests in the past dozen years and those of the biblical figure, Job. Job is represented in the Bible as a good family man who was beset with horrendous disasters that took away all that he held dear, including his offspring, his health, and his property. He struggled to understand his situation and began to search for the answer to his difficulties. God rewarded Job's obedience during his travails and restored his health and doubled his original riches. Job later sired seven sons and three daughters; however, his previous children remained dead.

Understand that in no way am I drawing this parallel between Job and myself because I consider myself on the same spiritual level or caliber of that biblical character. To the contrary! However, there are some similarities in Job's life lessons that exist in my situation and which I am seeking to understand.

Since 2009, I have lost: my health, my profession, my sense of identity, my income, my home in Sacramento, my aesthetic needs, my joy and purpose for living, the nearness of my grandson, and, most devastating of all, my youngest child.

Naturally the loss of Monique negatively impacts all of the aforementioned challenges. And naturally I constantly question why I had to lose her and why it's been so hard to recover from my loss. Most would say that I was a good person with a passion for my family, my profession, and the community. Maybe my lack of recovery is due to me failing the test that God put before me? Maybe there is no recovery from losing Monique.

Unlike my counterpart, Job, my faith did not grow in God during these difficult times. In fact, I cursed Him on many occasions for allowing my daughter to be murdered. These counterproductive thoughts still run through my mind from time to time. Fortunately, since the demise of my daughter, I have been rewarded with the addition of two beautiful, new grandsons and one gorgeous granddaughter, all blessings for which I am eternally grateful.

One of my previous pastors wisely and profoundly stated, *"If your God is not working for you, maybe you should try something else."* I hung on to that concept, and seriously had to analyze whether my mother's and her mother's, and her mother's mother's religion was really working for me. While digesting this idea, I think back to the poem I had written so much earlier, "Are You There?" And these lines strike me again:

Another test, another trial to test my waning faith.
The devil rejoices and makes me saith,
Are You There?
I need salvation, I need peace of mind.
I need to see a miracle, You, I want to find.
Are You There?
Fearful of living, Fearful of dying
No words are inspiring. No Angels are flying.
Are You There?
You said You'd never leave me.
You said my soul would be free.
Are You There?
I can't see you, I can't touch you.
I'm falling in an abyss of doubt.
Are You There?

It seems extraordinarily strange to me that once I lost Monique everything I respond to in life has become categorized as "life before Monique's death" and "life after Monique's death." The concept of religion and spirituality before and after Monique's death achingly burns at my soul.

My father was a pastor, so the ins and outs of the Baptist Church were familiar to me. My early personal experiences found the Baptist Church somewhat negative in nature—a lot of fire and damnation. When I lost Monique, good intentioned Christians would say things like, "Boy, a lot of bad things are happening to you." Or "Have you been going to church regularly?" Or "Are you praying enough?" I interpreted that their hidden messages were that something was wrong with me. That I had done something wrong for this horrific tragedy to fall upon my family. More guilt to contend with. At this time in my life, I just could not take it anymore. That is why I sought spirituality and happiness outside the Church.

I had actually first heard mention of SGI Buddhism on the big screen—in the 1993 biopic of the iconic Tina Turner, *What's Love Got To Do With It*. For years she suffered emotional and physical abuse from her heroin-addicted husband, Ike Turner.

Just as it happened to Tina, I was introduced to the practice of Buddhism by my own good friend, Daphne and began attending Buddhist meetings, but more so for the support group and friendship that is offered. Initially, I experienced a high level of culture shock due to my lack of exposure to the Asian culture as compared to the Black Baptist Church. But with the kind-hearted spirit and support of their members, I was willing to learn. Any spiritual discipline that teaches love, respect, a passion for education, and world peace, I can embrace. And I embraced the process of chanting *Nam Myo Renge Kyo* for absolute happiness even during suffering here on earth.

During my Buddhist faith exploration, we were taught the importance of living our lives courageously, like a lion in search of faith and truth. Currently, I am more like a lost kitten meowing weakly for a solid foundation; but I am working on it.

Having been raised on that "old time religion," however, it is difficult to totally ignore my upbringing. Living a faith-based life is an integral part of my DNA. Whatever a person's spiritual discipline may be, the important thing is *faith*. Life is so empty without it. I think of how empty life is without Monique; I cannot imagine layering a loss of my relationship with God on top of that.

And, I must admit, I began to miss gospel music and the energetic delivery of the gospel message from a spirit-filled pastor. Buddhism feels to me to be more laid back, nonjudgmental, and diverse with various genres of music being played at meetings—but no gospel music. Initially, that was not an issue for me, because during the earlier years of my grieving process, I could not listen to gospel music anyway. Way too painful. It reminded me of the betrayed I felt by the faith of my youth. But as the healing process continues, I have found myself more capable of listening to the music from my past.

So, along with my other spiritual explorations, I have begun to occasionally attend the Agape International Spiritual Center in Los Angeles. I like the positive empowering message from the pastor, Michael Beckwith, who has developed a culturally inclusive, trans-denominational atmosphere in his church, accepting Christians, Buddhists, Catholics, gays, lesbians, rich, poor, black, white, everyone.

The *mosaic effect*, of taking the most effective practices from spiritual disciplines that are aligned with my belief system, seems to be working for me at this time. It is all about love for myself, love for my fellow man, and staying connected to a cause greater than myself. Remarkably, my children have been very supportive of me during this process and the naysayers in my life have remained silent. They knew I was struggling to stay on this side, and my family and friends just wanted me to get better. By any means necessary.

CHAPTER 23

Moving Forward

WHAT I MISS MOST ABOUT Monique is her laughter. I miss the sound of her vibrant voice chatting about our family, telling me a joke, or excitedly sharing her plans for the future. I also miss that sultry, soulful, singing voice passed down from my mother through me to her. I will always hold in my heart the memory of her smile, the warmth of her embrace, the way her eyes lit up whenever she looked at that effervescent extension of herself, Jayden. As I write this, six *long* years have passed. And time refuses to move backward so I can hug her again.

What I love most about her was her boldness of spirit and tenacious strength. Monique was a strong Black Woman; she learned that from me. All my life I was strong. Until a single bullet brought me down. I know now, though, that Monique does not want to see me curl up and die in a pool of isolation and self-pity. *Stop all that damn crying, Mama!*

I still grieve and long for my daughter. The image of her face is the first thing I see in my mind each morning when I awake. That same image is there when I close my eyes at night to sleep. To awake and fall asleep daily with this sense of longing and loss is my paradoxical dilemma. Every day it is a struggle to keep from sliding back into that Black Hole of grief. Some days I am more successful than others. But that is the nature of grief.

The thing to know about Monique is that she thought about her future and her son's future. And even sensing the possibility that she might not live to see him grow up didn't deter her from always looking forward. Just the opposite. It strengthened her resolve. It caused her to take action and to plan ahead, regardless of what the future might hold.

When Monique came to me in a vision that day she was telling me that I needed to gather the strength to pull myself out of the Black Hole—for Jayden, for my family, and most of all for myself. If Monique could talk to me face to face right now, she would "Mama, you are part of something bigger than yourself. Now you need to go and find out what that is."

And so that's what I've resolved to do. And this book—this memoir of my life and my grief—is part of that effort to find something bigger than myself. If my sharing can help even one other grieving mother, sister, daughter, father, or son to know that they are not alone, not going, crazy, are not a bad person for the way they feel, then I've contributed something worthwhile.

As I hear the life stories of other victim's families who have lost loved ones to gun violence, I am encouraged by some of the great work many of those individuals are doing to make certain that no other family has this life altering experience. I am encouraged when organizations such as Moms Demand Action and Every Town for Gun Safety mobilize to effect change in gun legislation and to stand up to the powerful lobbyists of the NRA. Because I know that our societal infatuation with guns and violence are at the heart of a problem we seem unable or unwilling to solve.

I am encouraged when I hear top government officials willing to pass tougher gun laws that require extensive background checks to insure assault weapons, like the ones used in the shoot-out that killed Monique, are no longer in the wrong hands to commit havoc in our communities. I am encouraged but feel a personal and moral obligation to get up close and personal in this movement.

I know now that it is my mission to find a voice for Monique in the gun safety movement. I have determined that I must strive on her behalf to make a difference, not just for her son, but for all the children of this great nation when it comes to gun safety. By putting my grief into action is the only way I will be able embrace the words "Monique is gone but not forgotten."

Frankly, I am sick of feeling helpless.

As an educator, I know that a quality education is key to reducing the number of young people who participate in the gang culture; which in turn would positively impact the rate of gun violence. Many of the strategies that we implemented in our school such as mentoring, relationship building, value clarification, and simply giving youth the sense of belonging deters the need to join a gang. Our inner city youth need the skills required to make a living for economic power and hope for the future. They need to acquire the ability to positively interact with others, using their words to negotiate their differences instead of violence. This they get with education.

We need to hold our city, state, and federal officials accountable to institutionalize meaningful social programs with funding to be proactive in keeping children off the streets. We need a collaborative community approach working with law enforcement, families, and everyone affected by violence in the streets to make our neighborhoods a safe haven where even a thirty-year-old mother can have family pictures taken without having to sacrifice her life for her child. These are achievable goals. We know what to do, we just have to make it a priority.

To approach the issue of violence in our communities nationwide can seem quite overwhelming. The key is to break through the barriers city by city, neighborhood by neighborhood, family by family always keeping the mindset that failure is not an option when it comes to the lives of our children. When our children who are murdered become no more than a headliner for the news or another daunting statistic without action to change it, that's when we've given in to moral bankruptcy. Our motto must be: Never Give Up, Never Give In To Violence.

There is no silver bullet to quell the level of gun violence in America today. I just offer some possible baby steps through education to address this enormous issue that plagues our communities, affluent or not, today. And if all these proactive strategies to meet the social, emotional and physical needs still do not deter the youth of today from participating in a life-style of violence; then I say, "If you do the crime you should do *all* of the time."

It seems to me that across California hundreds of inmates are being released early due to let's-make-a-deal transactions behind the scenes between lawyers and the criminal justice system, criminal friendly legislation, age, good behavior, or to relieve overcrowding. I once mistakenly received an "early release due to his age" letter for one of the defendants in Monique's murder trial and he hadn't even served a year.

Unfortunately, the victim's family often has to take on the responsibility for the arduous task of monitoring the parole board to insure that the person responsible for the death of their loved one serves adequate time. I personally believe that since death is a permanent condition, criminals who have committed murder should serve their full sentences. A considerable amount of time by the jury and judge, as well as tax payer dollars, have been spent in the judicial process to reach a determination and penalty for the crime committed. To reduce the sentence is a travesty to the victim and the victim's family.

The defendants in my daughter's murder were all repeat offenders. If they were held responsible to serve their full sentences for prior crimes committed, my Monique would still be alive today. And so I say it again, "If you are so bold to commit the crime, then you should do ALL of the time."

CHAPTER 24

Final Thoughts

MY PHYSICAL HEALTH TODAY REMAINS a mystery to me. Ten years ago I had a ninety-five percent mortality rate with no hope of my enlarged heart becoming normal again. With all the stress and negativity that I have experienced on a daily basis these last six years, one would think my body would pay a costly toll. However, my heart has regenerated itself and returned to normal size with an infraction rate of sixty-five percent, up from twenty percent. The current regeneration of my heart is just short of a miracle. Unfortunately, there is nothing medical science can do to mend a broken heart of epic proportions when your child has been murdered.

Of course, I am challenged with minor ailments as all senior citizens are, but overall I feel great. I attribute my comeback to the concerned and knowledgeable medical staff, my level of discipline in following dietary, drug therapy, and life-style choices, and the Universe saying, "Hey, give this woman a break." My dear friend Daphne, who has so lovingly supported me during this journey, recently commented, "At times I've heard you express a desire to die, but you surely do take good care of yourself!" I have to laugh at that. My soul is full of gratitude for my good physical health.

My current spiritual beliefs are paradoxical, open-minded, a work-in-progress, and a very individualistic journey. I still question God frequently, but at least now we are talking again. As for reconnecting with religion, I vacillate between spiritual disciplines, taking the parts that benefit my life and applying the practices that facilitate me in my life at this time and in this space. There are concepts I embrace from Christianity and some from the

Buddhist practice. I choose to grasp the positives, the love for self and others, and the tenants aimed at making me a better person.

I continue to chant for the Three P'S—Protection for my Family, Prosperity, and Peace of Mind. I chant for a human revolution that transforms my negative Karma into a positive karma for my family, friends and me in this lifetime and future life times. I chant and pray for Monique to be free and infectiously happy in her new existence as she so respectfully deserves. There is no spirit more pure than a spirit that willingly gives her life for another human being like Monique did. She deserves the best!

Like Job I, too, am eagerly looking forward to the upside of life. Monique's murder has shattered my foundation. Now I must rebuild, not on my traditional past but on what really works for me and gets me through this journey called life.

Although my plan to help raise my grandson was altered by the reappearance of Jayden's father, Kenyatta, into his life, and by their subsequent relocation to Texas, I have no regrets in leaving Sacramento. I live near my daughter, Tamora. She has been my breath of fresh air and is that positive voice in my ear that keeps me on this side of Heaven. Another Unsung Hero in my life. I love her and her brother, Richard, so much. I realize now that each of us had our own journey to travel in order to heal and to arrive at some level of peace of mind.

One statement that Monique made in her last will and testament was "Of course my prayer is that I will grow old with my son or just to see him become a man, *but we just never know what tomorrow holds…*" After my baby's death, realizing how fragile life really is and understanding that we don't know what tomorrow or even the next second holds, I have made some life adjustments. These adjustments include how I respond to the people I love. I try to display more understanding than being judgmental, and appreciate every minute I spend with the ones I love, because it may be the last time we spend together.

I continue to text my surviving children; not a day goes by that I do not tell them I love them. In retrospect, many times I have needed the personal, positive affirmations included in these texts to make it through the day. A special thank you to my baby, Monique, for showing me the importance of never letting a day go by without telling my loved ones that I love them. Wish you could have benefited from the change in me that you inspired.

I think often about how Monique cherished her family and her friends. She and her best friend, Alethea, were so close that they even had their sons within three months of each other; and both boys' names were similar—Jayden and Jayce. In May of 2011 three-year-old Jayce lost his battle with brain cancer. He was buried within a hundred feet from Monique's mausoleum. In my spiritual mind, it brings me some comfort to believe that my Angel Monique was there to greet little Jayce, whom she loved and adored as her own son, when he passed over. Hopefully, Jayce is now safe in Monique's arms. Her love is that deep!

The evolving landscape of our family continuously moves toward love, hope and new beginnings. Proudly, I am glad to say that even though my children have experienced the unimaginable, they are still resilient and flourishing beautifully.

Tamora, is thriving in the film industry and is a life-long learner professionally and spiritually. The most illuminating characteristic about Tamora to me is that she exudes with positiveness and is a striking beauty in her own right. She is not afraid to live life and marches confidently to the beat of her own drum. Tamora is strong-willed and possesses a strong sense of responsibility toward others, which I so admire. If she has any vice at all, it would be a unique trait inherited from her mother called *shopping*! She believes that her baby sister, Monique, is omnipresent and is still actively involved in our lives, especially watching over her son, Jayden. A bright future with unlimited happiness awaits Tamora.

Richard, equally, has moved on with a new family of his own. He has remarried and he and his wife, Frances, are blessed with a son named Mateo and a baby girl named Maya Monique. Richard's oldest son, Rayonne, is an exemplary role model for his younger siblings by being sweet and being a triathlon athlete. Whatever sport Rayonne participates in, he excels. My son is a successful manager in state government and is always looking forward to his next challenge to conquer. Richard is an energetic and involved parent who showers his new family with love and devotion. He once made a comment to me that deeply touched my heart. He told me that he lives each day in an effort for Monique to be proud of him. Indeed, as Monique spies in on him from the heavens above, I can imagine that huge infectious smile of hers proudly and admirably shining on Richard because of the father her big brother has become. Richard has kept his baby sister's memory alive by naming his yacht "Big Roxxy" (Monique's nickname) and his darling baby daughter, Mya Monique.

Little Jayden, who is physically taller than all students in his classroom, always has and always will be the star of my show. The courage, tenacity and old man's wit that he has exhibited through his young life's journey renders me in awe of this little boy. He has lost like no child should ever have to lose; but on the opposite end of the spectrum, he has been showered with blessings that will enable him to optimistically face all of life's possibilities. Jayden already exceeds the expectations that his mother, Monique, and his immediate and extended family could ever have imagined. As of this writing, he still resides in Texas with the supportive, loving family Kenyatta and Keley have provided, and I visit as often as possible. Throughout each visit, I am a personal witness to the love, the emotional and physical growth that Jayden has demonstrated. He loves God and is thriving in school. While building wonderful memories with his immediate family, he respectfully and lovingly embraces the memory of the woman who made life possible for him twice, his mother, Monique Roxanne Nelson.

I wrote the following poem ten years ago for my children, and it may be appropriate now as I close out this memoir and this tribute to Monique.

<u>Freedom</u>
(By Deborah Nelson)

Freedom is a multidimensional thought.
Freedom can be experienced when we're together or apart.

The Last Portrait: A Psalm For Monique

Images of doves flying and people singing and full of joy come to mind,
Bells ringing, hope springing, and music playing from time to time.
But the concept of freedom means much more between you and me.
It is our signal that one of our spiritual souls has been set free.
When this day comes, no one knows the day or the hour.
However, the survivor must be strong and not allow their attitude to sour.
Yes, Freedom is a special place in time and space,
Where suffering and dying have no place.
Freedom is when you've earned the right
To walk the streets of gold and never grow old.
But the greatest delight
Will be walking in the Light
Side by side with the Holy One
Who gave His only begotten Son.
So Freedom can be experienced by all who know Him.
Yes, Freedom is our special word.
To signal each other that all's OK,
When we cannot express it in any other way.
Freedom is our way to hold on to the Love we shared
Here on Earth or in the celestial air.
There are no boundaries to the Love I feel for you
Because for my children anything I would do.
But when the Master calls
Every knee will bow and every tongue will confess.
On that day of atonement
We will truly be blessed
Not to say that the life we've known together as
Family won't be missed.

Per Monique's final instructions I have framed the last portrait taken of mother and son and displayed it in Jayden's room at my apartment for when he visits in the summer—and it is certainly huge. This photo depicts a smiling proud mother embracing her equally jovial two-year-old toddler dressed in a red and white Santa cap. The background setting of white, snow-capped mountains looks quite chilly and realistic until you notice Monique's sleeveless blue sweater. Something about the serene look on Monique's face and the surreal love in her eyes captivates me each time I study this picture—an image of tranquility and motherly love.

Sometimes, when I look up at her image in the portrait, I still find myself screaming to Monique not to leave the photo shop. Stay there until the pictures are developed. Just stay for five to ten minutes longer, and we can change the course of our lives.

The process of writing this memoir has been a long journey, reliving many personal and painful moments. But it has also been instrumental to my healing process and has helped me to refocus on a new meaning for my life. The one constant is love for family and keeping the memory of my loving daughter alive. I may be bent but I am not broken.

Someday I *will* write a poem about Monique. And when I do, it will be more than a poem—it will be a psalm, sung in praise of a mother's love and sacrifice that only God can fathom. Until then, let this book be my psalm for Monique.

Last Portrait

Monique, I wish you love—a love that transcends space, time, dimensions, galaxies, universes, heavens and even death.

Heart Strings

Family   Richard and Big Roxxy Yacht

Monique   Monique and Mom at Zoo

Kids At Thanksgiving   Monique and Jayden in New Apartment

Author, Deborah Nelson is a retired educator who dedicated her life to her family and the inner city school communities that she served. She currently resides in Southern California and has two adult children, four beautiful grandsons, and a granddaughter named Mya Monique after her aunt. Her purpose in writing this memoir was to keep the memory of her beloved daughter, Monique Roxanne Nelson, alive and to provide Monique's only son with information about his mother whom he will never have the opportunity to know. Monique made the  ultimate sacrifice on December 14, 2010 to protect her son from a barrage of stray bullets while gang members engaged in a gun battle at a public parking lot. Although this author's journey has been a difficult one, the joy is in knowing that her daughter's death was not in vain. Her grandson, Jayden, is adored by many and lives a life full of love.

APPENDICES

A. The Nelson Family Victim Impact Statement
B. Memo To Parkway Staff on taking medical leave of absence
C. Excerpts from Monique's Last Will and Testament
D. Kenyatta's Victim Impact Statement
E. Tamora's Victim Impact Statement
F. Resources For Families Who Are Grieving
G. Resources to Advocate For an End to Gun Violence

APPENDIX A

Victim impact statement for the Murder of Monique Roxanne Nelson
Friday, October 24, 2014

I am here to tell you about a vivacious, beautiful quick-witted young woman named Monique Roxanne Nelson. She was and still is deeply loved by a host of family and friends, but there was no greater love than the love she had for her rambunctious two-year-old son, Jayden. Since his birth, Monique worked diligently to provide for her child, made plans for their future and built a value system of family traditions that have been handed down from one generation to the next.

Monique and her immediate family had taken many annual Christmas photos at the One–Hour Photo Shop on Florin Road for a number of years. On Tuesday, December 14, 2010, she was proudly engaged in one of those family traditions by having Christmas photos taken with her adorable son. As she was waiting for her pictures to be developed and strapped her toddler in his car seat she was caught in crossfire of unspeakable violence that would devastate the lives of many for as long as they lived.

Without hesitation, Monique covered her only son with her body with a prayer in her heart that she and her son would be safe. Instead this heroic angel takes a bullet to the heart and bleeds out and dies in the arms of her two-year-old son. If it had not been for the brave act of his mother, this trial would have been about the death of a two-year-old child. The pain and anguish that little Jayden and those who knew and loved Monique experience on a daily basis transcends the meaning of tragic. To know that this story could had a totally different ending, if the defendants had made the choice not to engage in violence will haunt us for days to come.

Nothing good ever comes of violence. It is the great sadness of our species that we have not found a way to eliminate violence as a device to resolve our conflicts. Every act of violence brings us closer to death. The actions of the defendants on December 14, 2010 at Fly Cuts Barbershop have resulted in the tragic death of our beloved Monique Roxanne Nelson. Although it was not your bullet that killed her, the choices you made to resolve your conflicts with other gang members did in fact, end Monique's life. It was through unspeakable violence in a public place with the lack of regard for innocent bystanders and your lack of regard for human life, resulted in ending the precious life of a mother, a daughter, a sister, a family member and friend.

Do you truly understand the long-term effects this murder has made on our family; but most importantly on a six-year-old child, Jayden, whose greatest wish is just to see his mommy again? At the time of his mother's murder, he was only two years old. He is left with an indelible mark scorched into his consciousness of holding his mother's head while she lay dying and bleeding in his arms. This child is experiencing nightmares of bad guys with guns chasing him, has a severe stutter and is overly fearful of loud sounds and new environments.

He cries out for his mommy and we have to tell him that she is in heaven watching over him. It is impossible for a child or even an adult, for that matter, to grasp that concept when you need a mother's kiss, a mother's hug, a mother's encouragement and a mother's love here on earth. The center of his universe has been maliciously taken from him and will leave a void that no person can fill for the remainder of his life. The long-term effect of Monique's son being exposed to this level of violence and carnage is immeasurable. He will be in therapy for the rest of his life.

Monique was the golden spoke in the wheel that kept our family all moving in a positive direction. Monique now resides in a cold mausoleum for eternity. A senseless act of violence that did not involve her, her child, mother, father, sisters, brothers, aunts, uncles, grandparents' community and friends but has negatively impacted and forever altered all of our lives. A deep sense of unfathomable lost, helplessness and hopelessness is our new normal. Monique has become a dream deferred. The laughter is gone. Happy family gatherings are gone. Jayden's mother is gone. A daughter, niece, sister, family member and cherished friend are gone. Why can't the violence be gone?

Real loss occurs when you lose something that you love more than yourself. Only people who are capable of loving strongly can also suffer great sorrow. To the Nelson Family, Monique will die over and over again for the rest of our lives. Grief is forever. It doesn't go away; it becomes a part of you, step by step, breath for breath. We will never stop grieving the loss of Monique because we will never stop loving her.

Sooner or later everyone must sit down at a banquet of consequences for the choices that they have made in life. The defendants chose hatred and violence. Monique chose sacrifice and love. The defendants will go to prison for a still to be determined length of time. However, they are not imprisoned alone! Monique has received the death sentence and is paying the price for making the ultimate sacrifice on that tragic day. She has no tomorrows, no visitation rights and will never walk the face of this earth again. Her son, Jayden Butler-Nelson, has received a life sentence having to live without his mother and live with the memories of a day of violence that is etched in his young heart and soul. The Nelson family and friends have also received a life sentence of pain in trying to make sense of a senseless act that has left devastation beyond words and the experience of true joy a thing of the past. No one, the guilty or the innocent leaves this situation unscathed.

There is no closure for us. Whatever the sentence for this heinous act will not bring back our effervescent Monique. The sentence required by law will help to make the streets of Sacramento a safer place so no other family, friend or son has to experience this level of human suffering again.

The Nelson Family & Friends

APPENDIX B

December 3, 2009
To The Parkway Dream Team.

I hope this message finds you in the best of health and spirits.

The Holiday Season is upon us where global goodwill and well wishes are extended to all. I wish to express my heart-felt gratitude for the well wishes and the thoughtfulness that has been continually extended my way during my health challenges. It amazes me how one day you can be on a Caribbean Cruise out-dancing and out-eating all of the passengers on board and then the next day a mysterious case of laryngitis appears. Then three weeks later, it is determined that it is not laryngitis at all, but possibly thyroid cancer. Then, two weeks later you have surgery and thank God it is not thyroid cancer but a left-sided vocal cord paralysis that will require additional surgery in three months. During this problem solving process with the vocal cords, the physicians discover that you have a life-altering disease called cardiomyopathy, which is an enlarged heart that is working at 20-25% the capacity of a normal heart! I share all this personal and private information to reveal the difference a day can make.

Through it all, I am optimistic, getting stronger each day, and missing my Parkway Family immensely. A special thanks to the new administrative team of Jocelyn Moore and Rebecca Fuentes for "Keeping the Dream Alive" and maintaining high expectations for all. I also want to thank the Parkway Dream Team and especially my babies for continuing with our tradition of academic and social excellence in my absence.

All of my life, I have felt that I had to be a "Super Woman" and when I am given an assignment, ***I try to give it my all*** - emotionally, spiritually, and physically. To my chagrin, the physical component has taken its toll. My doctor's have placed me on a medical leave for twelve months to re-adjust my life style, try a series of new medications to treat my existing illnesses, and to me allow additional time to heal from a second surgery. Knowing my God and me, we can accomplish this feat in about six months. Oops, that is that Super Woman talking again. (Smile!)

Please continue to support, encourage, and love each other as a family with a relentless focus on stopping the educational failure for children of color and children of poverty.

My favorite song is "Everything Must Change." Although, I am unable to be with you physically this school year, know that my spirit and BIG heart beats in every inch of this school and most affectionately for my babies.

> *"Just like moons and like suns,*
> *With the certainty of tides,*
> *Just like hopes springing high,*
> *Still I rise!"*
>
> *Maya Angelou*

Happy Holidays and Expect the Best,
Deborah Nelson

APPENDIX C

The following is an excerpt from Monique Nelson's Last Will and Testament:

"If I pass before the date 07/06/2011 the money you receive from the insurance company will not be that much. I refuse anyone to go broke in this process. I ask you take the money and go to Morgan Funeral Services and cremate me ($600-$1,000) if you want a memorial service it ranges from $1000-2000 with the viewing of the body. There should be enough to cover that. If I pass after the date 07/6/2011 and you feel like burial is a better way to go. Then use my $20,000 (Not all of it) and prepare a nice service. Funerals are highly expensive. I'd rather you buy the casket from Wal-Mart (they sell them now☺) if it is possible don't spend more than $8,000 the rest of the money can benefit Jayden and that's its purpose. If viewing of the body is the way you choose to go, make sure "I'm fine as wine" The gospel song I want to be playing is "I'm Safe In His Arms."............Jayden also has a savings account. His account is *not to be touched!* When he gets a responsible age he is welcomed to his first ATM card. Make sure there is a decent limit on it. If he's 16 then no more than $50 a day. I am praying that whoever has custody of Jayden realizes the money is for Jayden Anthony Butler-Nelson's well being and not for your own self-gratification. If I have any belongings you can sell them or give it to the poor. (It won't be much)

It is MANDATORY that in Jayden's room he has a BIG picture of me and him by his bedside. And everyday you tell him how much mommy loved him and there's no greater joy than to have him as my son. I asked that you treat him, as he was your own son and give him all the love that he needs. Explain to him that death comes to us all. It's the end of one life But the beginning of another........Of course my prayer is I grow old with my son or just to see him become a man but we just never know what tomorrow holds. So I'd rather be prepared....You must do your best to keep Jayden with my side of the family. I only ask who has custody of him to make sure my son goes to church (involved in it) I think that's most important and will make him into a better man. If you're not involved that's fine, you can drop him off in the nursery or bible classes then pick him up. I would love for him to be in a private school But it all depends on the financial part, it's your decision. College is a MUST!

Written by Monique Roxanne Nelson

APPENDIX D

Kenyatta's Victim Impact Statement
September 2, 2014

Your Honor,

I am writing this letter on behalf of myself and my 6-year-old son, Jayden Anthony Butler-Nelson. Your Honor, Monique Nelson is the mother of our beautiful son, Jayden. I would like to share with you how a senseless killing has effected a little boy, who if had one wish it would be to see his mommy again. The mother who courageously paid the ultimate price for the love of our son by sacrificing her life for his. There is no greater love! My heart will always have a void knowing I will never see or speak to Monique again but your honor it's the void that I see in our son's eyes that hurts me more than anything. It's the times that I catch him gazing out the window or just daydreaming and I ask him "what are you thinking about?" and his simple reply "my mommy". It is truly painful to see a sweet little boy who is so young be in so much pain, anguish and yearning for a mother he will never see again. For a mother who showered him with all her love and for a mother who was the center of his universe. Jayden's life is and will forever be changed. I don't know exactly what he is thinking or what he feels but I do know he misses his mommy more than any of us can imagine. It's the look of hurt, confusion and total sadness that tears me up inside. We can be in the grocery store or watching cartoons and he will just start crying for his mommy. All I can do is hold him until he settles down and tell him his mommy is watching him from heaven. I tell him he has a mother who loves him more than anything in this entire world and she is with God watching him. It hurts me deeply knowing he will live with this void in his heart for the rest of his life all because of a senseless killing.

Monique did not have to die that tragic December day. I understand Monique's killer may not have intentionally killed her but the fact remains he took her life and potentially could have taken our son's life if it wasn't for her bravery. I ask you to hand down a sentence that will let the citizens of

Sacramento know the violence and killings of innocent law abiding citizens will not be tolerated. Let the punishment reflect a zero tolerance for criminals who show no regard for the lives of others, especially innocent children! I understand no amount of punishment will bring back our beloved Monique but I ask you to give the killer of Monique the maximum amount of years the law allows. In closing, your Honor, please take into consideration while deliberating a sentence that the killer of Monique may serve years in prison but Jayden will have a lifetime of heartache and a void no person on this earth can ever fill.

Sincerely,
Kenyatta Butler

APPENDIX E

Tamora's Victim Impact Statement

The Honorable Nicholas Haberman
Superior Court of California
County of Sacramento
720 Ninth Street
Sacramento, California 95814

Re: My Sister, Monique Nelson
Dear Judge Haberman,

It was a Tuesday afternoon, December 14, 2010 when I received a call from my older brother with news that I wouldn't wish on my worst enemy. It was a distinct tone that I've never heard from him before. He asked me to leave work immediately because there was something urgent that he needed to tell me. My heart stopped and I rushed out of the office, and on the way down the elevator my body went numb. I kept thinking what was so urgent that I had to leave a meeting and rush outside where he couldn't just tell me in my office. All these crazy thoughts were crossing my mind...was something wrong with my mother, did she have a heart attack, was there something wrong with my father, and the list goes on. I ran towards the parking lot to return his call. He proceeds to tell me that there was a shooting at a barbershop and that something happened to Monique. I immediately asked him what he was trying to say and started asking whether she is okay. He tells me that she is dead.

I fell directly on the ground and started screaming. Where is my little sis? I didn't believe him. I didn't want to believe him. This couldn't be happening. I rushed to the airport to catch the next flight out to Sacramento. I'm crying so hard that I can't breathe. The woman at the ticket counter kept asking if I was okay and everyone gathers around me pestering me with all these questions. I look at the television and there's a picture of my sister's body covered on the ground next to her SUV and my nephew Jayden in the arms of a firefighter.

It hits me that this is real. Never in a million years would I ever imagine that something like this could happen to my family. I watch the news all the time and hear sad stories of families that have lost a loved one, but this can't be happening. I just saw her on Thanksgiving. Then I can't hear anything. It's just silence and my heart is in so much pain that I can't feel anything. This was my younger sister. My only sister and she was the life of the party. She had all of these dreams of a better life for her and her son and one careless reckless event that didn't even involve her took her life away.

Nothing will ever be the same. I've never seen my dad break down until that day. He will never be the same. My mom will never be able to enjoy the holidays because without my sister it won't be the same. Jayden (her heart and joy) will never get a chance to see his mother again. She won't be able to see him graduate from high school or send him off to college. Although I try to be the light that keeps our family moving forward, I know that I'm not able to mend their broken hearts. My brother and I have lost our sister, my parents have lost a daughter, my aunt has lost a niece, and Alethea has lost her best friend. The thoughtless crime committed by Ronnie Smith has destroyed our lives forever.

Although we can't bring Monique back, it would at least help the healing process to know that justice was served and Ronnie Smith was to receive the maximum punishment. An innocent life was taken away. She was only thirty years old, your honor. She died protecting her son 11 days before Christmas. What better gift could she have given her son than to sacrifice her own life so that he can live? She exemplified what love really is, so we ask that an example is made today where people take responsibility for their actions and see that when you kill an innocent woman you will receive the maximum penalty. A life is gone and a family is destroyed. There are consequences for your actions and we pray that justice is served for my younger sister (Monique Nelson).

Thank you for your time,
Tamora Nelson

APPENDIX F

Resources For Families Who Are Grieving
Books:

- Bailey, Beatrice Toney, *Farewell, My Friend: A Step-By-Step Guide To Handling a Serious Illness and Even the Death of a Loved One* (Beatrice Toney Bailey, 2008)
- James, John W. and Friendman, Russell, *When Children Grieve* (Harper Perennial, 2002)
- Williamson, Marianne, *A Return To Love: Reflections on the Principles of A Course in Miracles* (Harper Collins, 1992)
- *I Wasn't Ready To Say Goodbye: Surviving, Coping & Healing After the Sudden Death of a Loved One* by Brook Noel & Pamela Blair

Websites:

- Compassionate Friends: Support for Families After a Child Dies www.compassionatefriends.org
- Julie Brams-Prudeaux, LMFT, Psychotherapy and Meditation Center, Encino California http://www.juliebrams.com/category/grief/
- Grief Recovery Institute https://www.griefrecoverymethod.com/

APPENDIX G

Resources to Advocate For an End to Gun Violence

- Moms Demand Action For Gun Sense (momsdemandaction.org/)
- EveryTown For Gun Safety (everytown.org)
- Sandy Hook Promise (www.sandyhookpromise.org/)

Made in the USA
San Bernardino, CA
07 April 2018